LOSING AMERICA: OUR NATIONAL CRISIS OF LEGALITIES VS. JUSTICE

How Our Own Laws Are Killing America
(Because We're Stupid and Just Too Damned Nice)

by

Imm d'Ceaze

DORRANCE
PUBLISHING CO
EST. 1920
PITTSBURGH, PENNSYLVANIA 15238

Dorrance Publishing Co
585 Alpha Drive
Suite 103
Pittsburgh, PA 15238
Visit our website at *www.dorrancebookstore.com*

ISBN: 978-1-6376-4348-8
eISBN: 978-1-6376-4660-1

With great appreciation to President Donald Trump and his family; broadcast media hosts Rush Limbaugh, Mark Levin, Ben Shapiro, Sean Hannity, Candace Owens, and Laura Ingraham; Former House Speaker Newt Gingrich; Hillsdale College and President Larry Arnn; Dennis Prager and all of his team and contributors; Glenn Beck and Blaze TV; The Heritage Foundation and its members; The Patriot Academy and teachers of Biblical Citizenship; Economist Dr. Tom Sowell; Supreme Court Associate Justice Clarence Thomas and his few truly conservative associates; Judicial Watch President Tom Fitton; NRA Executive Vice President Wayne LaPierre; Supreme Knight Carl A. Anderson, Knights of Columbus; Govs. Kristi Noem (S.D.), Ron DeSantis (FL.), Greg Abbott (TX); Ohio Rep. Jim Jordan; Sen. Ted Cruz (TX); and all leaders both political, private, and religious, and the many, many others that preach, teach, promote, and support conservativism and true American values. These are my heroes and they are the glue that is keeping America together.

RINOs and all others can go to hell.

CONTENTS

PROLOGUE

Beyond the Birth Certificate

I know it, you know it, and anyone that has an iota of logic (and pays attention) knows it. Even the Kenyans know it (https:// americanfreepress.net/barack-obamas-birthplace-a-tourist-attraction-in-kenya/).

And Obama knows it.

Obama is _not_ a native-born American and therefore he was not constitutionally eligible to serve as the President. The fact that Obama has spent millions to hide his school records, college records, birth records, and any other records that show his origin of birth proves it. It is simple logic that no amount of analysis, excuses, and intellectualizing can overcome. Period. Under great public pressure, Obama eventually released a copy of his birth certificate, but the first public Adobe computer analysis of that copy was conclusive that it had been altered and was blatantly fraudulent. Some dates, names, and places didn't even match.

He's also not a real American.

REAL American kids grew up playing sandlot baseball, shooting marbles, riding bicycles, digging holes for forts and playing cowboys and Indians or cops and robbers. REAL American kids played kick the can or hide-and-seek, or worked on farms or picked weeds in gardens or picked fruit in the orchards in the summer, rode horses, drove tractors, or chased chickens in their grandfather's chicken yard, and took their .22 rifles to plink tin cans or targets under the watchful eye of dad. A REAL American kid had lots of friends that remember him and the hot rod or old beater that he had as a first car—one he got all greasy from by fixing it himself. REAL American kids had great experiences with school sports, rock-and-roll dances, and military service to their country.

But I can't visualize Obama doing ANY of the things that I did as an American kid growing up.

Being *American* isn't just a matter of documentation. It's a matter of upbringing, of experience, of the DNA in your bones, and most importantly of patriotic attitude. I know foreign-born Americans that are Americans in their attitude and DNA, and others that are American ONLY by their documentation. Many of those "papered" Americans might have their citizenship, yes, but they aren't American in their soul. Obama belongs to the latter. Remember, attitude is as important as birthplace and experience, and that influences your political outlook and how you VOTE.

But the birth issue is now way beyond the personal fraud that Obama pulled off on the American people, and this new issue is much larger and more drastic and disastrous. The issue now is that Congress and the Judiciary must have also known that Obama was illegitimate.

And if you and I know it, how the hell could they not have known it?

And sadly, nobody in any branch of government did anything about it. This was the first significant, open disregard for the Constitution and the rule of law in our modern history.

In the face of this Constitutional fraud, the Congress that has the power of impeachment did nothing. The Judiciary that oversees our laws and serves as the watchdog for Constitutional infringements did nothing. And biased Judges appointed by Obama did nothing because they certainly weren't going to incriminate the very person that appointed them to a cushy, lifelong position, and the Congress is so calcified by years of cronyism that it is numb.

In the first half of Obama's first term when the Democrats were in the majority, although it was still unjustifiable it was at least understandable that they wouldn't impeach the star of their own party. But after Republicans won a majority in the House AND Senate during Obama's second term, what was the excuse? There is none. Article I Section 2 states that the House of Representatives shall have the sole power of impeachment. Perhaps the American people thought the election of a fresh batch of congressmen would have some positive effect, but there was no move for impeachment, and this writer would like to know why. Did the new congressmen instantly become numb and calcified in the corrupt stew of Washington, D.C.? As a majority, the new House should have immediately stopped all government action and demanded a resolution to the issue of Obama's Constitutional eligibility to hold the Office of the President. The citizens deserved to know and the Constitutional guidelines should be guaranteed. The validity of anything the fraudulent President said or did deserves to be proven, and that validity is vital. Virtually everybody wants and deserves to know. Good men in the military went to prison because of their doubt as to the validity of their Commander-In-Chief to order them to war. Law enforcement personnel were confused as to what to do and where to place their loyalties. They took an oath that means something to them, and it's an issue overriding every other issue, be it oil, war, the budget, or the economy. Obama's leadership (or lack thereof) was vital to everything else, and his Office should have at least been certified as legitimate in the climate of all this debate.

Remember, Bill Clinton was impeached not for his immoral sexual misconduct unbecoming to the Office, but for simply lying about it to Congress.

But look at Obama's history. On January 23, 2009, a mere 3 days after coming into his Presidency, Obama repealed rules implemented by G. W. Bush that restricted federal money for international organizations that promote or provide abortions overseas. And then another 3 days later he made an Executive Order to send $128 million from the U.S. Agency for International Development (USAID) to fund the International Planned Parenthood Federation and the Population Council, both of which are overseas abortion advocacy groups. What a great start at spending the U.S. taxpayers' money, signed late on a Friday night out of sight by any onlookers. The stage was set....

An embarrassment to most Americans, Obama bowed to foreign kings, sent cheesy gifts to our best allies, took over large private corporations, used taxpayer money to bail out private businesses, sent taxpayer money overseas for abortions, admitted thousands of potentially harmful Middle East refugee immigrants, sued one of our border states for enforcing our own national border laws, forced an unconstitutional healthcare plot down our throats, banned drilling for oil in our own country (while allowing and funding drilling for other countries), and appointed a plethora of czars to run the country while he spent millions of taxpayer dollars to take himself and his family on world tours. He (and his Sec. of State) supported U.N. schemes to control our privately owned guns. He is a known avid anti-gunner and has a clear record of supporting every bill that he ever had the opportunity to vote on to restrict our Constitutional Second Amendment protections. He took us to war in Libya without even thinking of notifying or discussing it with Congress. Just think—he talked to the European countries, the League of Arab States, the United Nations, and didn't even have the courtesy or respect to run it past <u>our own Congress</u>? And Obama has proven time and time again that Candidate Obama lied to the country in order to eventually be President Obama (so he could disrespectfully put his feet up on the historical desk in the Oval Office).

Unlike Obama, Clinton's personal immoral infraction didn't cost billions of dollars that we didn't have, spill the blood of our finest soldiers, use military weapons and equipment for the benefit of other countries that have a beef with Libya, and snub his own government bodies before unilaterally acting on an issue of world class proportions and implications.

And we impeached Clinton for a red-faced fib? That Obama's House of Representatives didn't impeach him is totally inexcusable and amazing! As one astute observer wrote big and boldly on his Tea Party public protest sign: Obama—<u>O</u>ne <u>B</u>ig <u>A</u>ss <u>M</u>istake <u>A</u>merica!

But as already stated in the title of this prologue, the issue is now more destructive and harmful and is way more important and beyond that of Obama's place of birth. That the Congress and Judiciary stood by wringing their hands while Obama took this country apart tells me that we, the American people, have lost the power of our Checks and Balances that was specifically engineered into our Constitution to assure that our form of government soldiered on even in the face of corruption in one of the three major branches. When any one of the three branches went astray, the other two could have the power to yank the other one back into line.

But that didn't happen. No branch did or even said anything to yank this wayward Administration off the path of destruction on which it began taking this country. It now appears that more than just one branch of government is corrupt.

And the American people and their way of life will pay dearly because of it.

I have preached for years that you can't blame anyone for trying to get a good job. Whether it's Clinton, Carter, Hitler, or Obama, you can't blame them for taking a highly paid job with lots of power and perks. The blame, and yes, I say blame, lies squarely on the shoulders of the naïve, politically unaware, historically ignorant, complacent, lackadaisical <u>voter</u>. Nobody in a position of public power in this country would be in <u>any</u> office if they weren't voted into it by the people. Nobody. And every single public employee at any level of government—city, county, state, and federal—takes an oath to support and protect the Constitution.

The supporting fact of voter ignorance, irresponsibility, and incompetence (while Obama took this country to pieces) was that way too many people still had "Vote For Obama" stickers on their cars years after he was out of office. And remember, Obama wasn't just voted into office for just one term. After seeing all of his corruption and incompetence and ignorance of America and disdain for the Constitution for four years, the voters even elected him for a second term, signaling that our nations' problems lie much deeper than just the voters (like poor education). The legislative records still show our elected officials voting to spend money we don't have, and trying to invent more ways to bolster the budget shortfalls in the face of a failing economy. And yes, sadly, these same legislators were voted into their positions by the voters, the general public that is naïve and ignorant as to where money comes from. It seems that most people, both regular citizens and elected officials at all levels, don't realize that there is no such thing as government property, government land, or government money. It is public property, public land, and public money, meaning that it belongs to the taxpaying citizens, not "the government." Government only oversees and manages the property, land, and money, but it all BELONGS to the citizens. And the citizens are collectively too stupid to realize that the money they don't have is being spent by someone else at the peril of our Nation's present wellbeing and that of our future generations.

Under Obama it appeared that we lost not just one branch of our government to lies, deceit, inaction, and unconstitutional corruption, but all three. Our national ship was not only without a Judiciary rudder, but without a Congressional crew, or Presidential captain. For the first time in many decades of this county's history I believe we were near the brink of national disaster. People were ready to take to the streets, prices were soaring, the economy was failing, national and personal debt was (and still is) overwhelming. We had an indecisive, un-American leader that criticized the patriotic (and peaceful!) TEA PARTY supporters, and yet we (collectively) had the arrogance, crust, and temerity to criticize other countries for their corrupt "Banana Republic" governments? What hypocrisy. Gold isn't at an all-time high for nothing. Under Obama this nation was failing and we were losing the faith and confidence of the rest of the world in the stability of our government, which is reflected in the value of our currency. Gold isn't necessarily getting more valuable; it's that our dollar is becoming more and more worthless.

This situation isn't just going to heal itself. It will take a great effort and will only be healed when the American voter finally wakes up and starts taking some lessons from history, starts observing the principles of our Constitution and its founding fathers, and starts thinking about all the socialist misinformation being peddled by the mainstream media. Until the American voter educates himself to where "government money" comes from, and educates himself as to moral, disciplined, political and economic principles, we'll continue this downward slide into the dismal pit of history filled with failed nations. We still have a town named Washington, D.C., but sadly there was no American government housed there, at least not truly American, until President Trump took office.

The Trump administration made us stop questioning whether our government is even still housed in the hearts of the American people, and he has given us hope for the future of America. He stopped our country from playing defense and kept our country from wasting energy by constantly putting out international brushfires. Trump switched to playing offense and put the communists, Muslims, Chinese, N. Korea, and Iranians (and Democrats!) on notice that it was going to be a different world as long as he was in charge.

God help us. And if we fail to overcome our problems, God help the rest of the world. Remember, about 400 years ago our immigrants fled from Europe and came to a primitive America to be free. But if we fail to keep our freedoms and national stability now in our modern America, just where will <u>anybody</u> go?

INTRODUCTION

After lying awake many nights agonizing in my Walter Mitty mind the horror that is s-l-o-w-l-y but <u>surely</u> happening in my country, I've tried to analyze just WHY America is on the brink of failing and collapsing as a country. And yes, it is in the slow process of failing, whether you see it or not or believe it or not—it's only a matter of time and your level of awareness. In spite of what all the academic analysts and media pundits say, I've come to the conclusion that plain and simple, collectively, we're just too damned nice, and it's our government and the Conservatives that are to blame. While the Democrats are brutal, lying, deceiving, and manipulative on almost all issues, the Republicans are honest, logical, and frankly, just too damned nice. The Democrats are great street fighters and will do whatever it takes to win, while the Republicans play by the rules—and they're losing. Trump was doing a great job at what he does, but the distractions forced on Trump by the Democrats kept him busy and distracted the rest of us, as a country, from doing the more important and long-range things that must be done.

While in their heart the overwhelming majority of the American people are honest, hardworking, moral, and ethical citizens patriotic to their country, they are way too busy with their jobs and families to pay close attention to what is happening right before their very eyes and literally right under their noses. Or perhaps they are aware, but nobody wants to upset the apple cart, make waves, or be the bad guy, and someone needs to have the spine, foresight, and awareness of our national danger to "fire the first shot." Yes, fire the first of many shots (figuratively speaking), in order to make a concerted effort to save our country from overwhelming chaos and invasions and irreversible undesirable changes. Some drastic changes are imminently necessary, and millions of citizens know it, feel it, and believe it, but nobody seems to know how to go about doing some very distasteful things that must be done to save our culture, heritage, freedoms, and American way of life. Nobody likes or wants violence, but it seems that our country is in denial. We know that some drastic actions—distasteful, violent, and destructive as they might be—*might* HAVE to be done, eventually, but nobody wants to take the first step. Nobody wants to fire the first (metaphorical) shot because there is no organization in place to sustain the effort needed to follow through after that first shot is fired. With a real gunshot, that one brave patriot would end up in prison with the political and legal climate of today. Some sort of "organization" is needed before the first shot is fired, and that is a massive problem. Just how will we get organized, and who and/or what will get us organized?

Collectively, we are in the situation of the frog placed in the cool water of a pot placed on a stove set to eventually boil.

We are getting killed slowly in ways that are not so immediately uncomfortable that we want to do anything drastic, but we're now to the point of either jumping out of the water or sitting still until we boil to death.

Ponder this concept because it is vitally important. Rapid change usually results in rapid reaction, whereas slow change is usually tolerated, even though the change isn't necessarily welcome. It's an insipid and insidious way for Muslims, illegal aliens, Socialists, and Communists to take over the country. Small steps at a time. As the temperature slowly rises in the pot. We are seeing it in the news daily both abroad and here in our own country.

Strangely, Americans are the first to shout about our convictions of freedom and quote our rights of free speech and freedom to bear arms, but on the other hand many citizens seem eager to give away those freedoms (mostly Democrats), like free speech and freedom to bear arms, in the hopes that the government will keep us safe, happy, comfortable, and well fed. And the government CAN do these things if we aren't concerned as to how it's done, how long it will take, what freedoms are forfeited, or how much it will cost; it's called Socialism. Issues abound, and we're so dedicated and obligated to swatting all the flies in Congress that we can't see the forest for the trees.

But America IS in a crisis and we need things done NOW. We are now more politically divided since the onset of the American Civil War, and we can't wait for the legal system to correct all the collective wrongs of the country. We're already a nation of lawyers (just look in the Yellow Pages of any phone book) but the legal system is overwhelmed and all but helpless to confront, control, or enforce the myriad of laws already on the books in the immediate crisis in which we find ourselves. The "wheels" of government are the existing laws, and although the grist is finely ground, it grinds much too slowly to avert the immediate crisis that we have. We're sliding into Socialism, and if you are one of the millions that don't believe we have a crisis you are not part of the solution, you're part of the problem.

So just what are the problems that have me (and 80 million voters) lying awake at night? In a word…

INVASIONS

First, physical invasions of people trying to get into our country illegally, from every direction on every border;

Second, invasions of foreign religious factions—such as Muslims—many of which are already in our country; factions whose ideology is totally contrary and counter to the traditional American culture, philosophies, morals, laws, and established way of life;

Third, invasions of political thoughts and ideals that are destructive to our freedoms, philosophies, economy, and future, not only from Muslims and other foreigners, but amazingly from many of our very own citizens, Judges, political leaders, and wealthy leftist billionaires; and

Fourth, physical invasions of lawless American citizens (and aliens?), paid for and inspired by leftists and socialists that, strangely, are also American citizens, that protest, riot, create civil disorder, and either want to "change America," or hate Trump, or both. And most of these people vote as Democrats.

Items One and Two (above) seem to be mostly assaults from outside of our country, and items Three and Four are mostly from within our own borders.

And like the chaos of war, all of these physical and intellectual invasions are occurring at once, making it a very tangled and complex picture of how to solve our problems and cure the National crisis in which we find ourselves.

INVASIONS OF ILLEGAL ALIENS

Everyone in America knows of the millions of illegal aliens that have taken up residence in America over the past decades, thanks to the lax enforcement and tracking policies of our government's Immigration and Naturalization Service. Until the age of communication and the age of massive and convenient means of travel, most of the people coming into America from all over the world were considered somewhat honest refugees, fleeing from oppressive countries to one of many opportunities and freedoms unrecognized in most of the rest of the world. Those that came to the USA were willing to embrace "the American way" and were anxious to work hard, assimilate into our culture, and speak the national, if not official, English language. And due to travel limitations at our borders, our border personnel were able to handle the workload to process the incoming aliens.

Those days are gone.

Yes, many foreigners are still honestly trying to immigrate like the previous generations, but we are currently not concerned about them. The ones we are now concerned about are the massive numbers that are coming to the southern American border to dilute our culture, change our culture, and replace our culture. And they aren't just coming from Mexico as most did in past years. They're also coming through Mexico from as far south as the South American and Central American countries, and into Mexico and Central America from the Middle East and other nations first to then go through Mexico and attempt to covertly cross into the U.S. And they are displaying a hostile temperament that belies their intentions. They are flooding across our borders carrying illegal drugs; carrying kidnaped women and children used for the sex trade; carrying pregnant women in the hopes of bearing babies as "natural-born" citizens due all the benefits of other Americans that have to pay for them; carrying ill-gotten cash intended for vengeful illegal use; carrying diseases of which we are unaware and transmitting it to our own innocent citizens; and escaping their home countries to escape prosecution from rapes, burglaries, and murder. Known gang members are also in these groups. Many illegal aliens are discovered and apprehended only *after* they've been caught for committing a heinous crime and then are found to have previous criminal records that would have prevented the authorities from allowing their entry if only the officials would have known about them. Newspaper stories abound with articles of criminal activities, rapes, and murders, and not just from one incident, but of many aliens which were repeat offenders with criminal records a mile long, and who seem to be in a "revolving door" of catch-and-release instead of being deported, punished, or imprisoned. Our own INS, border agents, police, and politicians know this, and previous administrations allowed it. Trump wanted to build a wall for a relatively small sum of five billion dollars to keep out illegal aliens, and yet it was opposed by the Democrats, while the estimates for the costs of having illegal aliens on welfare, in hospitals, on food stamps, in jails, and in the prison and court systems was estimated to be costing about $155 billion. How could Democrats oppose the expenditure of $5 billion to build a border wall but allow the country to suffer the cost of illegal aliens to the tune of $155 billion? It makes no real logical sense.

And remember, aliens of *any* status are only a problem if they're **IN** <u>OUR</u> country. As long as they stay even one foot away from our border, technically and legally, they are the responsibility of either Mexico or Canada. Our responsibility begins when aliens actually enter our country, so the way to keep our costs down for healthcare, welfare, food stamps, the court system, law enforcement, prisons, drugs, rapes, murders, and burglaries is to simply keep them on the other side of OUR border. Logic screams that we need, desperately, to "Build the Wall," and NOW, but the liberals and Democrats oppose building a border wall, even after declaring in former years, in front of Congress and on the news, that they too believed strongly in reinforcing our borders.

Simply because of their dislike for Trump, the Democrats have changed their previous stand on this critical issue. They are hypocrites.

Trump's administration was so busy playing defense, it could hardly focus on its offensive game. In spite of these conditions Trump's accomplishments were amazing.

Democrats are killing America while I lie awake at night wondering WHY.

And to make matters worse, thanks to former President Obama, our own political officials were putting restrictions on our law enforcement agencies for punishing the illegals that were apprehended. What kind of national insanity is that? Americans are supposed to obey and respect the law, and yet some of our highest elected politicians have voiced their opinions that we need to be "compassionate" to the oppressed masses wanting to come to America for a better life. That might make some sense if those same illegal invaders were carrying American flags and testifying their allegiance to us. But no, they carry their own national flags, shout "Death to America," and burn, stomp, and defile our American flag. And as they shout their epithets in their native language they wonder why we don't welcome them with open arms.

To the aliens: If you really want to improve your conditions, stay in your own countries, work and study hard, and make the changes needed to better your <u>own</u> country instead of coming to America to suck off the largess of the American welfare system, funded by our hardworking taxpayers. America is already in debt to the tune of almost $30 <u>Trillion</u> and you're likely to jump out of the proverbial pot into the frying pan. So stay in your own countries, make the needed improvements, and BOTH of our countries will be better off.

And while you're at it, get it soundly planted in your minds as to where money comes from—it comes from the energy, creativity, inventiveness, and work of people; not a cent comes from "the government" because there is no such thing as "government money." The "government" is a conceptual thing, not a physical thing, and the only legitimate money in the country is owned and supplied by the taxpayers. "Government money" only comes from the money that the government first confiscates from the citizens who originally earn it from their work, inventiveness, and creativity; all the government is, is a distribution system to put money where it wants, at the benevolent expense of those that actually earned it and then donate the money elsewhere, courtesy of the Congress and the Internal Revenue Service. Even the money printed by the government printing presses is ultimately owned by the public, and the more money the government prints, the more it devalues the currency already in circulation that has been gained from meaningful work, inventiveness, and creativity. Until currency is actually legitimately earned by someone in an act of work for goods or services, and channeled through the appropriate outlets (like banks), it is essentially counterfeit and has no value. That very concept is why counterfeiting is illegal.

The same goes for government property. "Government property," whether it is land, buildings, or supplies, is PUBLIC property, paid for and owned by the citizens. The federal employees and politicians are making the government work, but they are only temporary cogs in the big wheels of the conceptual government. The government employees and politicians are only managers and stewards of the public property, not the owners of it. The land and buildings are permanent fixtures, whereas the government employees and elected officials all come and go, eventually, leaving behind only their legacy. But the "government property" stays with the taxpayers. So when aliens start to use America's "government money" to pay for their subsidized food, housing, healthcare, etc., they are only killing the country to which they have come to find a better life, at the expense of someone that works for a living. It's like killing the goose that lays the golden eggs.

It's been said by many that the true metric of how desirable a country is, is to measure how many people are trying to get

IN to a country versus how many are trying to get OUT of a country. And as it concerns the countries south of our border, just because they have trouble in their country isn't a reason that we should flood them with our money to solve their own problems. Countries south of the U.S. should organize their own economic and political structures and systems to entice and motivate their own citizens to stay put. And if they can't stay put, we should have a border wall and enforcement personnel strong enough to repel them so that they'll want to go elsewhere other than America, unless they want to do it legally, openly, and by the book. Americans should be compassionate but we don't have to be stupid.

So the illegal aliens are invading with a vengeance, and nothing effectively lasting is being done about it. WHY? Try our own homegrown American Socialist resistance for a start. The Left has been reading the Marxist playbook for years.

It's a documented fact that a lot of the aliens sneaking across our thousand-mile unfenced and open borders are NOT just from the countries to the south (or north) of us. The border patrol apprehends many that have previously come from other parts of the world that are labeled OTMs—Other Than Mexicans. OTMs can be from anywhere and are probably more important from the standpoint of being a National threat to our security because of terrorism, international spying, or a whole host of other intentions. Overlooking a bunch of these OTMs could end in results similar to the 9-11 disasters that killed over 3,000 innocent people in 2001 and cost billions of dollars of damage to our economy. And remember, it was found that those deadly terrorists had been in America for a long time, planning, training, and practicing just how to pull it off. We know they are still here by the thousands, and are making concerted efforts to kill us in one way or another, physically, culturally, religiously, or politically. Check out some of the largest cities now, and you'll see that the Muslims occupy large tracts of territory that even the police are reluctant to enter or patrol. Again, we thank our very own national policies and agencies that have allowed it to happen. And about half of the American liberal population and government legislature think nothing about it. They are either ignorant of the onerous threatening changes, or are supportive, or just plain lackadaisical about the issue and couldn't care less. Too many politicians and government workers are just happy to keep a good job. These are the same officials that swore an oath to support the Constitution and protect America from all enemies "both <u>Foreign and Domestic</u>." Such short memories they have unless they are outright liars and hypocrites (which I believe many are). Remember, <u>ALL</u> government and military employees take the Oath, so many Conservatives suspect it is intentional that the Democrats and Liberals simply "look the other way" about these critical issues that are damaging our country.

In early 2020, a 2019 news article reported that 1800 illegals breached the El Paso, Texas, border sector <u>in just one day</u>, and it estimated that 71,000 would breach the border there by the end of April 2019.

One of the most stunning recent announcements is about groups of citizens trying to form militias to aid the border authorities, but were turned away by the FBI and other government entities.

The border agents are being overwhelmed, but didn't accept or want the help of our own militia citizens? Are they and we just stupid or what? More about that in the following pages.

INVASIONS OF MUSLIMS

The Islamic chaos, destruction, murder, and mayhem has been going on for decades but nobody wanted to target Muslims or admit that it was 99% due to Muslims that were responsible for the terrorism happening all over the world. But the attack on our home ground that occurred on 9-11-2001 was a wake-up call to most Americans that there were some drastic flaws to our policies and methods concerning immigration and National Security. In those first days after 9-11 there was a national solidarity about the love for our country, flag, and all things American. Flags flew from every pole and edifice in sight. Yet it was only a matter of days until the finger-pointing began: it was the fault of the President; it was the fault of Conservatives that already hated Muslims due to the incidents of the multitude of bombings and beheadings; it was even the fault of the crowd that believe in conspiracy theories that it was planned by our own government. Some complained that we were attacked by the Muslims because "we weren't nice to them and they took offense." Unlike the National Will that was demonstrated by the vast majority of the people that volunteered to fight the enemies in WWI, WWII, and Korea, our enemies were now some of our own citizens, pointing fingers at everyone that had opposing political views. Political parties have always had differences, but the divisions in our culture really began festering during the era of the Clinton administration when everyone jumped on the bandwagon of observing "political correctness," and it only got worse from there. We shouldn't say anything that will hurt someone's feelings, especially to Muslims, they said.

Ironically, one of the best speeches from Bill Clinton during his Presidency was one on the vital importance of limiting immigration, deporting illegal immigrants, tracking and deporting alien criminals, etc. The crowd cheered loudly at the proposal during Clinton's speech, but how times have changed. Again, the record is clear about the hypocrisy coming from the modern Democrats, supported by the mainstream media.

To this day countless conservative citizens that closely followed the campaign of Obama and the stomach-turning policies that he implemented, still believe with conviction that Obama was an illegitimate president because he was not a Natural-Born citizen. Obama sequestered (and still has) ALL of his history of personal experiences, birth records, school transcripts, and anything else that could show that he was not Constitutionally eligible to be seated as the President of the United States. And yet the Democrats and Liberals totally ignored the facts that the people in Kenya were giving praise to him and building memorials to him as being the first foreign-born president. And yet the Democrats ignored the vetting process leading up to his election. And yet the Democrats ignored the policies implemented during his eight-year tenure that allowed $150 Billion to go to the American-hating Iranians for building nuclear facilities, while he apologized to countless dignitaries and leaders of other countries for the behavior and success of America.

One of the most shocking experiences of my life was the day when I heard that Obama had won the Presidency. I (and millions of other voters) was, literally, speechless for a whole day, pondering what the future held in store for America. My saddest day was the second day of Obama's Presidency when the new President is traditionally given his National Security briefing. Thinking of all the military secrets being given to a person that nobody really knew (and we still don't really know) turned my stomach into knots. Many Americans even dismissed as an oversight the missing American Flags traditionally lined up on the stage behind the podium in several of Obama's earlier speeches. Hmm....

When I was employed in the Federal Government I regularly received copies of the Federal Register, the official record of the government's activities. In the Federal Register I noticed that one of the first actions recorded about Obama was his gift from the American taxpayers of $128 million to be used for abortions in a foreign country. Off to a good fiscal start for a new president, huh, being careless with the money of the taxpayers sent to foreigners. We now have public records of all his huge expenditures that drove our National deficit to nearly $20 Trillion, while he and First Lady Michelle and the kids took lavish vacation trips all over the world, and as Obama played golf and arrogantly put his feet up on the historic desk in the White House while he was relaxing. All at the expense of the taxpayers, you and me.

Several clandestinely produced videos of Obama admitting the origin of his Kenyan birth to small select groups eventually surfaced on the internet but were mostly ignored by the fawning general public faithful to the nation's first president of color. Also, because he attended a Christian church for years, he claims to be Christian, but many of his actions and speeches videoed at Muslim political rallies strongly indicate that he is/was a "closet" Muslim. He has stated as much in close company on videos leaked to the public, and after all, his early childhood years were spent studying religion as a Muslim. It's been said by some that he nearly "remodeled" the White House at the beginning of his presidency until he and his advisors wised up to the fact that Muslim decor didn't present a good image to the majority of Americans. And recall the passages in the Qur'an about deceiving the infidels until you have the advantage to behead them.

Our awareness about Muslims was intensified and well publicized by the events of 9-11-2001. By 2016, wars in the Middle East against radical Muslims were happening in many places, so during the public grilling of all the Republican presidential candidates prior to the 2016 elections, one of the press interviewers posed an important question to be answered by each and all of the candidates on the televised stage. The interviewer asked: Just how would you handle the Muslim terrorists in the Middle East, and exactly what would you do? The answers came down the line from each of the candidates, with each bloviating and pontificating as to how they would proceed, implement tactics, strategies, and costs, and wordsmithing as fast as they could to demonstrate their best ideas and intellectual prowess. When it came to former Speaker of the House Newt Gingrich, Gingrich answered with only two words:

He clearly and purposely spoke—"Kill them."

The stunning honesty of his two-word position made him my favorite candidate; his two distinct words summed up a thousand thoughts on the subject by millions of political Conservatives. His solution was simple. His solution was impossible to _mis_understand. And his solution was the only lasting solution, believe it or not. On that note, be sure to read to the end of this writing.

Over the past decade the USA has spent billions of dollars, countless weapons and military supplies, and gallons of American blood to kill the many (but relatively few worldwide) of the 1.5 billion Muslims in the world. Their long-term mission is to eventually dominate the entire world. It's in their Qur'an and they are often seen at rallies on television proudly voicing their intent and progress towards their goal. They are the enemies of America and have openly vowed to destroy America no matter how long it takes, and we've heard it from the leaders of almost all the Muslim-dominated countries in not only the Middle East but also all over Africa, where the Muslims slaughter with impunity all the non-Muslims, and especially Christians (which gets little or no coverage from the mainstream press). We see the protests and foreign flags and posters saying "Death to America" in Europe and our own major cities, several of which now have official Muslim Day parades. All this while we're trying to kill them all across the Middle East. And then what do we see happening in the USA, all courtesy of our own government? We see neighborhoods where the local home-grown citizens are displaced to make room for imported Muslim "refugees" that are given transportation, subsidized housing, subsidized food, education, and healthcare, and even allowed to build Mosques on ground that was formerly homes to regular Americans. Just how blatantly ignorant and stupid can we be? Even in our own military, here on U.S. bases, we have had Muslims in our uniforms open fire and kill numerous U.S. soldiers on military bases in order to satisfy their goals. Why would any logical military official allow Muslims to be in our military service? You can't trust them if they are Muslims because their self-professed mission is to wipe out all infidels, so it would seem totally irresponsible to allow Muslims in our military. Am I missing something here?

Again, we're just too damned nice, and I'm losing sleep over it.

Has America totally lost its common sense? Has America lost track of the history of how we came to be the most prosperous, wealthy, successful, and most powerful country in the world? Our success wasn't just by being nice to our enemy. And ironically, on one hand we kill as many Muslim radicals as we can overseas, and on the other hand we bring Muslims to America and support them here on our own soil! Talk about a conflict of interest.... Has America totally forgotten how to fight for our freedom and way of life, or are we just going to roll over and bring more Muslims here so they can impose Sharia law on us?

Bringing sworn enemies into our own country isn't the way to win the war. Maybe we should have just forgotten the Revolutionary War, Civil War, WWI, WWII, Korean War, Viet Nam War, and all the wars fought in the Middle East over the past 20 years. We might as well have, because now our own government has brought war to our own shores and cities with the help and aid of those that want to kill us and have vowed to dominate us no matter how long it takes. Nationally (and militarily and strategically) we are thinking ahead to the next few years, decade, or the next election cycle, while the Muslims are thinking ahead to the next century! We seem to have forgotten the words of General George Patton when he said that our soldiers won't win the war by giving their lives for our country;

we'll win the war by making the other poor bastards give their life for THEIR country. That was then, but now we're just too damned nice.

The indisputable facts of the statistics of our birth rates in our country (and many of the other developed countries) guarantees that we'll eventually be overwhelmed by the Muslims. Traditional Americans are not reproducing themselves to adequately sustain our culture. Obviously the Muslims are already the prominent religion in the Middle East, and we are now in the process of seeing their domination efforts in Europe, Africa, clearly in America, and actually all over most of the world. And they aren't about to stop on their own without massive efforts on our part to maintain our American culture. Islam is now the fastest growing religion per capita IN AMERICA, especially among the minority races. In about 20 years it is projected that there will be enough Muslims to elect an American president and Prime Minister of Canada. Frankly, I believe that Europe and Africa are already essentially lost causes, and it's only a matter of time when America will pay the price of our government's own stupidity and blindness to the threat of Islam.

So it begs the question, WHY? Just why do we ignore the threat to our country and do absolutely nothing about it? Yes, it's unreasonable and impossible to rid the entire *world* of Muslims, but it is still reasonable and doable to rid the Muslims from American soil if only we could find the National Will.

Think of Israel, a small country, surrounded by countries that vow to annihilate them, and yet they survive attacks and assaults constantly. Why? Because their population is consolidated in their beliefs and National Will. And while the U.S. has strong agreements to aid in their defense against all the aggressive

Muslim countries surrounding Israel, we allow Muslims into our country. How can we be supportive with money and military power to fend off Muslims in Israel, and yet welcome Muslims to immigrate here? Are we blind to the history of what is happening to Israel while we open our country to the Muslims that want to immigrate here? It makes no sense. It's illogical. And stupid.

Consider this recent article published by an internet news service on January 4, 2021, by trendingrightwing.com:

Muslims Home Raided By Agents... What They Discover Sends Chills Down Their Spines

"The Muslim Brotherhood is out to destroy America and the rest of the North American continent from within. While your liberal friends might laugh this off as just a far-right conspiracy theory, it's something that we conservatives have suspected for many years now. The big difference is that now we actually have the evidence to back up this behavior from Muslims.

"Law enforcement agents recently raided the Annandale, VA home of a prominent member of the Muslim Brotherhood, and this led to the discovery of a blueprint detailing the thirty-year plan for Muslims across America to engage in a complete takeover of the North American continent. Of course, now that the cover of the Muslim Brotherhood has been blown, you can bet your bottom dollar that they will stop at nothing to cover it back up again. However, it's up to us to fight back. Our children's lives depend on it.

"First of all, a little backstory might be in order. Twenty-seven years ago, the leader of the Muslim Brotherhood, Yusuf al-Qaradwai, first traveled to America. His goal? To organize Muslims throughout America about the ultimate plan, which was to engage in a complete takeover of the United States. The plan had a thirty-year timeline.

"Indeed, one of the most effective elements of this plan would be a tactic called 'Muruna,' which is a strategy that allows Muslim to violate strict Sharia law so that they can convince Americans that they are not a threat to them and are just like us. Nothing to see here, move along. Naturally, there is no question that Muruna has been extremely effective, moving about just like an Ebola virus and allowing Muslims to stealthily integrate into every aspect of North American society.

"So, it's out in the open now. We know the truth. The radical Muslims have been planning this all along. Thus, we don't have an excuse now. Simply put, we must fight back. We must show our children the true meaning of what being an American is all about, because if we don't, you better believe that the Muslims will show us all about their ideology, and if we aren't careful, there will come a day where we will collectively look in the mirror and not recognize the reflection looking back at us. Here are the steps in the takeover plan for these radical Muslims:

"<u>Phase One</u>: The establishment of a discreet and clandestine leadership plan.

Like other secret societies, obviously they are not going to tell anyone about the first phase of this plan. "

"Phase Two: Gradually appearing on the public scene and engaging in several different public activities. Needless to say, they were highly successful in the implementation of this stage. For example, they had various important and nefarious goals they wanted to meet during this time frame, such as the infiltration of different sectors of government. They also wanted to gain the trust of senior scholars and religious institutions and receive public support and sympathy. They also wanted to establish a shadow government alongside the real government, and yes, they have been largely successful in that as well.

"Phase Three: Escalation

In this stage, the Muslims will continue to bend the society to their own will by utilizing mass media.

They will do this just prior to outright conflict and confrontation with the powers that be. This is the stage that we are currently in.

"Phase Four: Completely open and public confrontation with the government through exercising a myriad of political pressures, including an aggressive implementation of the above-mentioned approach. Domestic weapons training, various overseas activities, and other activities in anticipation of the zero-hero.

"Phase Five: In this last phase, they will seize power in order to fully establish their Islamic Nation in every aspect of this nation. All parties and Islamic groups will be united together.

"Of course, this is their overall, general plan. However, the document that was seized in this raid shows that they have taken some very chilling organizational steps to see this Islamic movement to its fruition. They have solid operations, planning, mindset, and vision for each and every step. Simply put, we are dealing with a truly organized enemy. Some of the extra details are as follows:

- Making the Muslim presence larger by such things as birth rate, immigration, and refusing to assimilate;
- Occupying and dominating physical spaces;
- Controlling the language used in describing the opposition;
- Making sure that everyone living in the "Muslim Community" completely follows it;
- Making sure that non-Muslims never study their doctrine (Sharia);
- Being sure that Sharia law is complied with even on local levels;
- Fighting back against counter-terrorism efforts;
- Intentionally subverting any given religious organization;
- Utilizing a strategy known as "law-fare," which is the use of the suing as a weapon;
- Demanding accommodations or claiming victimization;
- Condemning "slander" against Islam;

- Infiltrating the U.S. education system;
- Demanding the right to practice Sharia law practically anywhere;
- Confronting Western society and denouncing their laws and traditions; and
- Demanding that Sharia law serve as a replacement for Western Law in all jurisdictions.

"This plan has literally been three decades in the making and we are just now getting aware of it. Of course, I'm sure liberals will say that we are overreacting, but there have been plenty of other things we have turned out to be right on, how do they know we won't be right on this as well? Not to mention the fact that Muslims have flown under the radar in this country, but all the while they were just building their arsenal and simply recruiting more to their evil ways.

"Is it any wonder that President Trump has been trying to implement a travel ban from countries that are known to support terrorists? As this raid clearly shows, the clock is ticking, and the time to act is NOW, before we end up like Europe."

Evidently my paranoia is well founded by at least one of our astute law enforcement agencies; hopefully our Department of Homeland Security is keeping track of these radicals.

After WWII when the scattered Jews were given the opportunity to go to their traditional "Promised Land" they were few in numbers. But they had faith and hope (and really no place else to go) so they quietly began immigrating to Israel, growing their numbers, improving the harsh arid land in Israel, and buying land from the local Arabs, both Jewish and non-Jewish. They displaced the Arabs slowly but surely, until the Jews ultimately became modern and industrial, developed technology, and finally developed nuclear energy and nuclear weapons. They did this slowly and gently by imposing laws and regulations on the Arabs that were unfavorable to the Arabs and the Arabs went out of Israel willingly. Smart move. We Americans should do the same to the Muslims—prohibit the construction of mosques, prohibit Sharia law, ban further Muslim immigration, and insist on the Muslims denouncing Islam or get exported to a mid-Eastern country of their choice.

And we will not win a War of Attrition with the Muslims not only because of their rapid birth rate while our birth rate is stagnant, but also because of the tactics used in their terrorist methods. On 9-11-2001 a dozen enemies of the USA sacrificed themselves to kill over 3,000 of us, with billions of dollars impact to our economy. One of our own Muslim military soldiers killed many of our own soldiers on our own base. A few Muslims recently killed over 300 and wounded 500 in Sri Lanka. A single Muslim in a truck runs over dozens on a street sidewalk. Their human and economic cost for killing us is minimal, while our human and economic costs are maximized. It's a smart move for them. By contrast, America spends millions of dollars for an aircraft and bombs to kill just a handful of the radicals.

While we stew in the boiling pot like unknowing frogs.

Remember the old TV advertisement encouraging motorists to frequently change their oil and filter? The greasy guy said, "You can either pay me now, or pay me later," implying that the oil and filter change now was cheaper, easier, and made

21

better sense than neglecting the task and having to replace an engine later for a lot more trouble and expense. Should we do it now while it's cheap and easy, or wait until everything self-destructs and the cost is overwhelming or unacceptable? That is exactly the situation with America and the Muslim presence. We can have some chaos now and "clean house" in America, or we can wait another decade or so and have a massive Muslim problem for which correcting it will probably destroy our entire country. France and Germany are essentially lost and intimidated; let's not let it happen to America.

Whether right or wrong in hindsight, Roosevelt gathered and sequestered all the domestic Japanese in America at the outbreak of the war with Japan for a lot less justification than we have now concerning the Muslims. The Japanese were completely gentle and decent non-threatening citizens compared to the openly hostile Muslims that cling to their loyalty and to their Islam flag and philosophy. Any war anywhere is bad, but war in one's own country seems to be horribly damaging and long lasting in the memories of all involved. A modern war soldier can just come back from being thousands of miles overseas and forget that it ever happened. But with a civil war on U.S. soil, families and neighbors will see and experience the horrors about the same way as the soldiers.

> Quotes: "*If you must break the law do it to seize power; in all other cases observe it.*" And, "*I have always reckoned the dignity of the Republic of first importance and preferable to life.*" And another, "*Never give your enemy a small blow.*" —Julius Caesar, about 52 B.C.

In WWI it was said (rumored) that Black Jack Pershing once captured about 50 Muslim enemies, dipped bullets in pig blood and shot 49 of them, allowing one remaining Muslim the chance to go tell others as a warning. Author Mark Perry (Aug. 20, 2017) refutes the story as false. But true or not, the authenticity of this story isn't the issue. The issue is that the message is the same as right now, today. We need to stop being so damn nice and do to the enemy what they would be happy to do (and <u>are</u> doing) to us and others around the world.

General MacArthur had many patriotic quotes, such as **"War's very object is victory, not prolonged indecision. In war there is no substitute for victory;** and **"It is not of any external threat that I concern myself but rather of insidious forces working from within which have already so drastically altered the character of our free institutions— those institutions which formerly we hailed as something beyond question or challenge—those institutions we proudly called the American way of life."** And **"Americans never quit."** And **"It was close; but that's the way it is in war. You win or lose, live or die—and the difference is just an eyelash."**

I strongly suggest you re-read and remember the above part about "prolonged indecision" and "insidious forces within" and ponder what is happening right before our eyes. Don't be in denial.

And now President Trump comes along and the chasm between the parties only grows wider as the rhetoric from the Democrats grows more acrid and aggressive. Numerous Democrat congressional leaders that in the past were <u>filmed</u> making fevered speeches to close the border to illegal immigrants; proposing to dedicate massive amounts of funding to build a wall to thwart invasions from illegal immigrants; fund and support our immigration agents to stop illegal drugs and criminals from entering our country; and impose other logical and feel-good policies, are now vehemently <u>opposed</u> to these same protective measures, mainly because the Republican President of their opposing Democrat party is getting done all the things that the others only talked about. All these actions by Trump to help make our country secure are logical and legal, but still the Democrats now oppose these efforts and policies. The Democrats have been "speaking out of both sides of their mouth." So it begs the question: WHY? Half of the liberal Americans are even responsible for the uproar about Trump putting restrictions and bans on Muslims immigrating to America, and the pressure of the mainstream media is unbearable. Amazingly, most of our own mainstream press is complicit in the ongoing destruction of America.

In April 2019 the iconic church of Notre Dame burned during the Christian Holy Week between Palm Sunday and Easter, even after officials testified as to all the precautionary measures in place to assure the fire safety of the process of reconstruction of the roof. Interestingly, in 2016 there was a report of vans parked close by that were found to have explosives with Arabic writing on them. And on Easter Sunday 2019 in Sri Lanka eight coordinated bombings occurred in churches and tourist destinations that the Health Minister Rajitha Senaratne said were already known to be targeted by terrorist groups as early as April 4. Police even had names of the ones behind the plot, and Senaratne blamed a local Islamic group for the attacks that killed over 300 people and wounded over 500.

At the beginning of March, an illegal Muslim immigrant tried to burn down the Saint-Sulpice church (http://www.leparisien.fr/paris-75/paris-l-incendie-a-l-eglise-saint-sulpice-n-etait-pas-accidentel-18-03-2019-8034678.php). At mid-March, an illegal Muslim immigrant tried to burn down the organ of the Saint-Denis basilica (another jewel) and destroyed stained glass (http://www.leparisien.fr/paris-75/paris-l-incendie-a-l-eglise-saint-sulpice-n-etait-pas-accidentel-18-03-2019-8034678.php).

On Twitter, thousands of Muslims were rejoicing and saying that they are happy that Notre Dame was destroyed! (http://www.fdesouche.com/1192185-sur-les-reseaux-sociaux-des-musulmans-lient-lincendie-de-notre-dame-au-tweet-blasphematoire-du-jeune-hugo-la-veille)

Notre Dame burned during Holy Week 2019, and eight churches and tourist destinations in Sri Lanka exploded. While Muslims cheered. Coincidence? I'm sure the liberals in denial won't see any coincidence, but others concerned with the future of America surely will.

What we have here is an assault on Western Civilization. Clearly. The conflicts between western thoughts and philosophy are as old as the ancient Greeks and the Middle and Far Eastern cultures. With the birth of Christ and the development of Christianity, those differences only increased, with the significant difference being that Christianity is based on love, peace, and tolerance, while the perverted Islamist development 620 years later believed in killing, destroying, taxing, and subjugating everyone that disagreed with their religious philosophy. The two philosophies are as conflicting as oil and water; they just won't mix and can't possibly mix due to their vast differences.

As a refresher to their beliefs and philosophies, let's review the following from the Qur'an "bible": 3:28 Muslims must not take infidels as friends; 3:85 Any religion other than Islam is not acceptable; 5:33 Maim and crucify the infidels if they criticize Islam; 8:12 Terrorize and behead those who believe in scriptures other than the Qur'an; 8:60 Muslims must muster all weapons to terrorize the infidels; 8:65 The unbelievers are stupid; urge the Muslims to fight them; 9:5 When opportunity arises kill the infidels wherever you catch them; 9:30 The Jews and the Christians are perverts; fight them; 9:123 Make war on the infidels living in your neighborhood. (The messages above have been abbreviated and shortened, and I've seen different versions and texts of the Qur'an that "soften" the harsh statements above, but the overall messages are the same.)

Heard enough?

So now with the vigorous onslaught of the West perpetrated by the East we are placed in the situation of kill or be killed; live free or live under subjugation; temporarily abandon our philosophy of love and peace and fight—and WIN—or be taxed, subjugated, or beheaded. We've seen it on television and various websites—the Muslims lining up their infidels and slitting their throats and beheading them. Graphically and proudly. We saw the captured American airman bound in a steel cage, burned to death in public. We've seen their mobs screaming "Death to America" and heard their declaration of war from sources in both America, Europe, and the Middle East, but we don't react as if we were at war. They'd behead us in a heartbeat, so why is it so unspeakable that we should do it to them? Have we totally lost our will to fight back?

To many pseudo Americans, the rounding up, deportation, or imprisonment of Muslims sounds obscene and brutal. But I say NO; public beheadings and public burnings are obscene and brutal. Get some perspective.

So which will we choose?

It's our choice and it's not too late to save America, but delaying only makes the outcome of the West vs. East conflict more difficult and less predictable. Personally, I believe that it is already too late to save several of the European countries due to the number of Muslims already inside their borders, mainly Germany, France, and Britain.

At this point, we could discuss the current and long-time pervasive invasion of other offshore nationals, like the Chinese, Middle Easterners, and others that have ensconced themselves into our universities and workforce. Just remember the two Americans uncovered in the 1950s that were caught spying for the Russians. Julius and Ethel Rosenberg were American citizens who were convicted of providing top-secret information about radar, sonar, jet engines, and nuclear weapons, and at that time the United States was the only country in the world with nuclear weapons. Convicted of espionage in 1951, they were executed in 1953, being the first American civilians to be executed for such charges and the first to suffer that penalty during peacetime. Only two years passed from capture to execution. A just and speedy legal procedure.

These days it seems that America has forgotten how to deal with spies.

INVASIONS OF POLITICAL THOUGHTS AND IDEAS

President Ronald Reagan said it best about the government trying to fix problems when he quipped that government can't solve the problems because government IS the problem. And government certainly is the problem because of an ignorant electorate that votes into office ignorant candidates that claim to have all the solutions and answers for/to all the dummies that have no ability to think for themselves. And yes, I'm talking about the Democrat party and its liberal and socialist followers. We are currently being bombarded by political thoughts and ideals that are clearly socialist in nature by newly *elected* young invaders that have little or no meaningful experience or expertise in politics, government, or knowledge of (or concern for) the U.S. Constitution. And some are Muslims and outright self-proclaimed Socialists.

What was once a party that believed in government involvement in some ways that were (admittedly) needed, today that same Democrat party has in reality now evolved into the Socialist party, regardless of what they use as a name. Russian "Light" now, but becoming bolder and stronger by the minute. We even have numerous avowed self-proclaimed Socialists already in elected political positions, where in the past only a token number of voters would ever vote for a known Socialist. They've now come "out of the closet" and are actually winning positions. Yes, Socialists are winning votes and political positions in the AMERICAN Congress.

From Prager University:

*Radical socialist ideas are spreading like wildfire through the younger generations in America. The majority of Millennials (those born between 1981 and 1996) identify as socialist. Nearly **70% of Millennials** support a government-funded, "Medicare-for-all" healthcare system.*

*The "Green New Deal"—a radical environmental policy proposed by socialist Rep. Alexandria Ocasio-Cortez—**is supported by more than 50% of Millennials.***

*And **49.6% of Millennials and members of Generation Z** (those born between 1996 and the mid-2000s) said they would "prefer living in a socialist country," according to one poll.*

According to the *Washington Examiner* (May 2019): A new poll from Georgetown University's Institute of Politics and Public Service indicates that, unless we act quickly, our nation is headed for the brink of disaster. The poll found that while a majority of voters believes that "everyday civility" is on the decline, a similar majority believes that their political leaders should double-down on their special interests and refuse to compromise. (In shorthand: Unless things change, we're headed for a Civil War.)

Over the decades, the Democrat party has manipulated educational systems, Teacher Unions, and curriculums that have doomed our nation to failure because they have been so ready to abandon some of our most precious laws and ideals. In too many schools young children are no longer taught to re-cite the Pledge of Allegiance to the flag, and when they do there are pressures to eliminate the words "under God" that recognize that there are more forces in action than those mortal ones we encounter daily on this earth. Without the constant reminder of the Flag and what it represents, the history of our nation is shuffled aside or swept under the rug and forgotten, and the significance of the huge amounts of blood that was shed to secure our freedoms and way of life are diluted. The leaders of our teacher unions seem more interested in salaries than the teaching of courses in ethics, civics, religion, morals, American and World history, and the Constitution. So at voting age, the young people now have no clue as how to make sound decisions or engage themselves in critical thinking whenever they venture into the voting booth and the world of politics.

Make no mistake, it was designed and engineered by the political Left many decades ago so that Socialism would, in time, be the end result of our educational ignorance. And half of our people have swallowed those doctrines hook, line, and sinker. The other half are waging the good fight for American traditional values and they proudly label themselves Republicans or Conservatives.

A little history:
The Democrat party was formed in 1792 under several names and versions, and appears to have been formalized during the Presidency of Andrew Jackson in the 1830s.

Then in the early 1900s an ideological movement in the U.S. started when about 100 people met in New York and organized the Intercollegiate Socialist Society (ISS). Chapters were established on over 60 college and university campuses coast-to-coast, and in time the directors of the movement explained that the ISS was set up to throw light on the worldwide movement of industrial democracy known as socialism (*The New York Times*, Jan. 28, 1919).

By 1921 violence associated with the USSR had given the term "socialism" a bad name, so ISS decided to rename its group "The League for Industrial DEMOCRACY." Of course the term is deceptive, and in 1928 the U.S. Army Training Manual (No. 2000-25) even went so far as to describe the differences between a democracy and a republic in their original and historic sense (*The 5000 Year Leap* by W. Cleon Skousen).

James Madison evaluated the historical record of democracies, stating that

> *Democracies have ever been spectacles of turbulence and contention; have ever been found incompatible with personal security or the rights of property; and have in general been as short in their lives as they have been violent in their deaths* (Federalist Papers, No. 10, p. 81.).

(In other words, you can vote yourself *IN* to socialism, but you have to shoot your way *OUT* of it.)

But in the end, it seems that by design, the Democrats named their party because it sounds like democracy. Similar words and sounds, so similar meaning, right? And Democracy sounds great as a concept, but it only works in small geographic areas, not vast territories like states or countries. So, carelessly educated people buy into "democracy" totally unaware that our founding fathers did NOT form a democracy as our political system, but founded a Republic ("if we can keep it"—said Ben

Franklin) where groups are represented by elected officials. The modern Democrats seem to have little respect for the basic foundations of our national Constitution and are so unaware of its meanings that even many lawyers, legislators, and judges seem to have no real working knowledge of the Constitution. Otherwise, why would the many city, county, and state governments and councils, at every level, continue to chew away at the Constitutional protections for gun ownership? It is a law placed in the highest, most basic and foundational legal instrument in the history of the world, i.e. our written Constitution. Gun ownership isn't an option or a right to be granted or denied by the government or the laws of men; it is a "Natural" right, given by God and recognized and protected by our Nation's Constitution. The language of the Second Amendment even makes it clear where those rights come from. And Democrats seem to love the idea of speech that is polite and "politically correct" even as it impacts our freedom of speech.

And is justifiable killing okay? Of course it is. People defend themselves, armies kill their enemies, cops kill bad guys, the courts execute hardened criminals, and innocent babies are murdered daily. Whoa! ... wait?! Babies killed? Daily!?

Now to make it clear about the issue of abortion, it is widely understood that there are unfortunate and uncontrollable instances of chemically caused birth defects and/or rare genetic defects that are known to be 100% lethal to either the mother and/or baby. These medical complications must be dealt with by the doctors to save the mother, and perhaps abortion of the fetus is the only choice. But these kind of abortions are ___not___ the issue. The political "abortion issue" is one of killing perfectly normal babies simply to appease the wishes of the mother for her selfish convenience. They call it Pro-Choice for the mother, and the hell with the infant.

The legal killing of humans by the gladiators and lions in the Coliseum was a great spectator blood-sport during the Christian persecutions by the Romans 2000 years ago, so let's compare it to the present times.

Let's put the setting in, say, a football stadium, packed with 60+ thousand spectators, screaming and shouting at the spectacle and entertainment of the football game. At the halftime we could bring out a pregnant mother on the verge of delivering a baby while lying on a table, and at the center of the field, right in front of the thousands of spectators, we could have some officials scramble the brains of an infant right on the brink of birth and dump the bloody mess into a basin or even on the ground— all televised, of course—close-up on the big screen at the far end of the stadium, and broadcasted to the millions of people in the TV audience in their homes. Or better yet, just for the drama, we could let the birth be completed and then just set the infant aside to gasp and fend for itself while lying on a table, for all the spectators to see. Of course the clock is clicking down for the second half to begin, so to hurry the process we simply let one of the officials step on the infant's head—spewing blood, brains, and all—or stepping on its chest to crush the life out of it, still televised and in plain view of the mother, the officials, the spectators, and millions of television viewers at home. A great blood-sport, really no different than the Roman gladiators and lions slaughtering the Christians 2000 years ago. It seems we haven't refined our social and cultural tastes much, huh?

This paints a sick picture, and it is repulsive, obscene, disgusting, and stomach-turning to even think of writing these words. But if this contrived image of the bloody, brutal, slaughter of an innocent, helpless, perfectly normal infant doesn't turn your stomach, just what the hell will? *The dismemberment of live babies still in the womb is real.* The Democrats say abortion should be allowed, but I would suspect that only the coldest heart or deranged mind would say it's okay to kill a baby in public, even if it was less bloody (like suffocating it) if they were to view it themselves, in public, on the big screen, and broadcast on TV. While hundreds or maybe even thousands of Christians and others might have been publicly murdered by the Romans, literally *millions* of unborn American babies have been killed—*legally*—by the liberal Democrats that had the power to enact such laws.

But on one hand, there is apparently a huge disconnect in their intellect and logic that allows Democrats to know that abortion is murder, while on the other hand they'll still vote to approve it (unless they're just plain ignorant of human biology). I suspect the difference is that murder is okay if someone else does it, and *if **YOU** don't have to see it happen*. Murder witnessed in mass public is a repulsive social, political, cultural, moral, ethical, and legal no-no, but behind the closed and hidden doors of a clinic or hospital murder is evidently okay for Democrats, and even for the Supreme Court that allows it. Game laws for hunters even prohibit killing an infant fawn deer, but it's okay to kill a human baby. Priorities? Perspective? Anyone...?

Why would judges at the highest levels in our land allow the slaughter of millions of perfectly healthy babies killed by abortions right up to and including the moment of natural birth, even at the moment of its first breath? And worse (if it can be any worse) even after the viable baby is out from its mother and lying on a table while someone debates what to do with it? The very idea is sickening to a moral person. It's the Democrats that are clearly leading the way on this issue, when any moral, ethical, and logical thinker would readily conclude that life begins at conception, not just somewhere later in the nine-month period of gestation. It's simple; the male sperm encounters a female egg and it might or might not result in fertilization. But if a cell is dividing, a future baby is alive, and we all know that as soon as a sperm cell enters an egg the zygote begins dividing. Dividing=alive. Not dividing=not alive. And what is really distressing is that many Christians, including some Catholics, vote for Democrats, knowing full well of the Democrats' stand on the issue of abortions. (Hypocrisy and stupidity are alive and well....) And by the way, President Joe Biden and House Speaker Nancy Pelosi are (or claim to be) Catholics. They (and many other Christians) are double-standard hypocrites.

It's all due to a lack of knowledge (or lack of caring) of religious, moral, ethical, and Constitutional education, taught over decades to those unable to engage in priorities and critical thinking. We've lost our "moral compass" and our sense of right and wrong. Democrats want to save a dolphin or whale but allow the killing of human babies. Just the destruction of the eggs or embryos of many endangered species of animals can cost the offender tens of thousands of dollars, but what is the cost imposed on the murder of a perfectly normal human child still in the womb? Nothing. Not a dime. Zero. Not even a penny. So abortion is legal, but is it just? Hardly. (And remember, the little person in the womb has no voice in the matter.)

*"Our Constitution was made **only** for a <u>moral and religious</u> people. It is wholly inadequate for the government of any other."* –John Adams

There isn't even a slap on the hand for killing what is estimated to be a million babies a year that could be potential doctors, lawyers, workers, and legitimate taxpayers supporting families, schools, churches, and our national budget.

Under the guise of the right to privacy assured by the 14th Amendment, in its 7-2 decision of Roe vs. Wade on January 22, 1973, the Supreme Court overturned a ban on abortions in Texas that opened up the rest of the country to permit abortions under certain guidelines. At 1 million abortions per year for the past 48 years an estimated <u>50 million</u> babies have been killed. Our cultural birth rate is already below the statistical standard of sustaining our people, so we unthinkingly make matters worse by allowing "legal" abortions. Is this sound Liberal thinking or not? Again it begs the question WHY? Are we just too free to do some of these things, or are we just plain stupid? And immoral. And unethical. And unjust. We are killing our own, while the Muslims are busy growing their population. While the softies in the Humane Society whine about the many dogs and cats that need help, our wounded and disabled Veterans get ignored. I believe we have a warped and misplaced sense of priorities. Evidently, widespread legal abortion falls into the pigeon hole of "if I don't see it, it doesn't exist."

After Obama said that he had campaigned in all 57 states (yep, he said all 57), in one of his speeches he stated that America was no longer a Christian nation. Really? Reminders are visible everywhere of the Christian religious American values and beliefs instilled by our Founding Fathers: carvings on our public buildings of Moses with the tablets of the Ten Commandments; statements from God on our government legislative buildings; and "One Nation under God" in our written flag salute. And you can't miss the thousands of Christian churches scattered all over our American cities and towns. And has anyone taken notice lately of the National motto clearly stated on every penny, nickel, dime, and dollar of our National currency that says "In God We Trust"? Yes, that same currency that is the standard for value equivalency *around the world*. At this point, readers need to query the internet at The Patriot Academy and read the history of America's Christian founders. Note especially their course offered on "Biblical Citizenship" that will cement the argument about our national religious heritage.

Obama obviously has a myopic and narcissistic view of himself and America. The Presidency of Obama greatly damaged the structure of America, but thank God, America's decline and damage was arrested and mitigated by Trump.

> *"Only a virtuous people are capable of freedom. As nations become corrupt and vicious, they have more need of masters."* – Benjamin Franklin

So who will protect these established American values? Who is patriotic enough to turn the tide that we see destroying—daily—our National and cultural values? Just who is willing to "fire the first shot" to preserve America? Just who, what, and how will we organize an effective resistance to the cultural, political, and physical invasions?

An invasion of our thoughts and ideas has come about in the way of surficial things to make us all feel good at the expense of logic. For instance, Gun-Free Zones are a way to make you "feel good" when you believe that a sign is going to protect you from gun-wielding maniacs entering a theater, school, night club, or airport. How many articles in the newspapers have disproven that fallacy over and over again? Shootings in schools, theaters, and other populated places occur when there is no one to shoot back, plain and simple. Yes, there is no way to prevent someone from slipping in to shoot up a congregation at prayer in a church, but a few members being shot before a good guy with a gun shoots back sure beats *nobody* shooting back, resulting in the wanton slaughter of a whole group of innocent people. Local sheriffs admit that the police can't be everywhere, and when it takes less than one minute to kill a roomful of school kids in a classroom, it takes five minutes for police to respond and get to the school. Sorry, too late. That one violent minute is past and the police are only there after the fact. Conclusion: School officials and teachers should be armed. Perhaps how they do it and go about it is up for discussion, but what is not up for discussion is the fact that "No-Gun Zones" are a farce. A "feel-good" thing for the liberals that puts everyone at risk. And what about the post-high school students attending our colleges? They are of voting age and many are eligible to have concealed-carry permits, but most colleges and universities ban guns from campus, and at night that puts the young women in particular, at risk. Except for military and law enforcement folks, *Nobody* is ever forced to carry a firearm, but it should be a personal choice for the responsible honest citizen. Remember, four airplanes full of passengers, billions of dollars of buildings, and thousands of people died in the terrorist attacks of 9-11-2001 because no one had a firearm to kill the bad guys. And what did the terrorists use as weapons? A box knife. Think about that for a while, digest it, and tell me something logical about preventing the honest citizens from carrying guns—honest citizens that have been fingerprinted, background checked, and trained in the safe and proper use of guns. Or at least arm and train the pilots or crew. After seeing several hijackings of aircraft, someone proposed the idea of "Licensed Gun Carriers Only" on a newly planned airline. I don't know if that ever took off (pun intended) but the thought is sound.

Another "invasion of thoughts" is the exclusive idea spawned by Liberals that we shouldn't say certain things. Well, yes, in some cases concerning safety (like yelling FIRE in a packed theater as a joke), and perhaps being polite in a relaxed social setting so as to avoid a ruckus in a nice restaurant. But the liberals have gone way too far when they blame something bad on the results of what they call "Hate Speech." Even the concept grates on my interpretation of Free Speech.

First, hate isn't a crime, it's an emotion and a feeling. Saying "I hate" something (you name it—people, broccoli, traffic jams, etc.) has probably been spoken by every person on the planet at one time or another, and it has never been considered a crime. It's a modern fabrication of liberals. Crime is what occurs and originates from committing bad physical behavior and actions. Oh, yeah, the lawyers and wordsmiths will bend things into "libel" if reputations suffer a financial hit or an embarrassment to their intellectual property or academic or professional standing, etc., but what is creeping into our English lexicon is a single additional word that is politically motivated to make a legitimate physical crime worse by tacking on the feelings about it, usually motivated against one kind of "believer" against another of a different belief. Thanks to the Liberals, the invention of the term "Hate Crime" is heard (and distributed by the mainstream press) when a person of one race kills or assaults a person of a different race. All of a sudden a crime isn't just an old-fashioned crime, it is embellished with the "Hate" attached to make it seem more egregious and awful. But it's really a mystery to me that when a Black kills a Black he isn't charged with a Hate Crime, or vice-versa when a Caucasian kills another Caucasian (or any other race). So why does the "hate" make a crime any different? Again, the lawyers and liberals will talk about intention, as if the victim gives a damn if he was liked or disliked as he bleeds to death and dies, or if it makes any difference to the family. Does the element of hate on the part of the offender mean he should get a lighter sentence if it was just a plain old-fashioned murder, or should he get a harsher sentence because of his "feelings" when he killed the other person? Again, the wordsmiths and lawyers will find something clever to say, but to many it's a ridiculous and superficial way for the liberals of a specific political group to get their "pound of flesh" and mileage out of anything publicized in the newspaper for some political advantage.

The real issue about the inflammatory word "hate" is the polarization that it causes between politically and culturally different groups. Again, the whole end game of the Liberals, Socialists, and Democrats is to "divide and conquer," and highlighting a crime as "hate" between different races, religions, or political groups is a great way to further their agenda.

And Judges and Juries (of all people) fall for it, and worse, they and the mainstream media even continue to promote it.

UNCONVENTIONAL WARFARE

Make no mistake, this country is engaged in an internal war, but unfortunately only one side is making any progress toward its goals. The two sides are the "Right" and the "Left" but at this stage there are no uniforms to distinguish just who is who. By day most of our citizens look like conventional Americans, mixed together as a variety or races, religions, languages, manner of dress, etc. But by night the radical Left (presently ANTIFA and Black Lives Matter) is beginning its quest to destroy America and the laws and values that make America AMERICA. The Left wants to rewrite history, erase our history, and replace our history with the ideals and standards of Marxism and Socialism, as if their plan will make America better. Or as if tearing down or defacing a historical statue will actually alter the truth of history. The history of Marxism, Socialism, and Communism has been shown to be a dismal way of governance by the powerful towards the average citizen. The most obvious result is that these "–isms" destroy the middle class, leaving only the (relatively) few powerful and wealthy upper class, with a remaining huge lower class that suffers from poverty, loss of freedoms, and a lack of the standard needs of life.

So as we find ourselves in this unconventional warfare, I believe the construct of the plan is as follows:

Without uniforms and weapons, how do we distinguish the good guys from the bad guys? It's easy really—the _good guys stand around and watch_ while the bad guys burn stuff, invade buildings, break windows, overturn cars, destroy real estate and businesses, and steal goods from the stores. Even the best of the good guys, i.e. the Police, are being ordered by some Governors and Mayors to let the anarchists "run their course" while the Police and news photographers stand around and do nothing to counter the mayhem. Does this sound like good governance? The obvious answer is a resounding NO! So, it begs the question as to just why there isn't a resistance to the anarchy?

Again, as said numerous times previously, Americans are just too damned nice.

And here's how the unconventional warfare is conducted:

First, we see that the anarchists are doing damage, invading businesses, and burning cars and such, **_but they aren't armed._** And herein is the flaw in being tolerant by the "good guys."

As long as the anarchists are <u>unarmed</u>, the Police (or National Guard or Militia or Military) are reluctant to shoot the offenders because our own Legal System would go berserk over it! The lawyers would have a heyday with authorities killing "unarmed" people—that are American citizens—anarchists or not. In the daylight, the Constitution would be used to hammer the Law Enforcement authorities to a pulp, while by night the anarchists would simply continue trashing our most beautiful towns and cities. Note that most all of these cities are under the governance of Democrat Mayors and Governors. Anyone that hasn't noticed this is blind to reality. And remember also, that no politician in any elected office is there on his own; the ignorant and uninformed Democrat and leftist <u>VOTERS</u> PUT THEM THERE.

So the Unconventional Warfare is succeeding as long as the anarchists remain unarmed and are not shooting at the Police or other authorities.

But does the fact that the anarchists are unarmed justify the leniency by the armed Police, Militia, or Military? Should the armed authorities simply set beside their stack of armaments and watch, while the cities continue to be raped, burned, and ransacked night after night? Should all these public crimes be ignored? If so, for how long? Most logical and sane citizens will say **No** to these questions, and the time to stop these crimes of violence and destruction is NOW.

Action NOW is much better than action later. Like in the Dirty Harry movie where he says that "shooting people is okay, as long as the right people get shot!" That's an entertaining cliché in a movie, but this is real life and at this point the future of our country might depend on some of the right people getting shot by our armed authorities.

But again, we're too stupid and just too damned nice to shoot unarmed anarchists. Consider the issue of what is legal vs. what is just. It's time that justice is served, or we WILL lose this country, like it or not or believe it or not.

LEGAL VERSUS JUST

What we have here are issues about what is <u>legal</u> versus what is <u>just</u>. There are many aliens coming to America legally, taking their turn, standing in line, willing to undergo the background checks to assure America that they are disease free, honest, and capable of working to the betterment of America, and willing to make an effort to speak our language, fit into our culture, and assimilate as best they can to our American fabric. Being legal is good, and it is also safe for them and America to be "documented" so that we can afford them the protection they deserve as humans and legitimate Americans, and to assure to the existing Americans that these are good people legitimately trying to make a better life and be good future citizens. It is not only illegal but unjust for other aliens to sneak across our borders to derive the instant benefits of America when so many others before them sacrificed so much to get where they are or want to be—legitimately.

The liberal crowds shout (believe?) that it is inhumane and unjust to prohibit the illegal aliens from entering our country because of their humanitarian concerns. But the same liberals and Democrats are quick to forget what a border represents, and the risks to our country that come from not documenting who is in our country and the reasons they want to be here. For a start, crime, drugs, terrorism, disease, and human trafficking come to mind, as well as the dilution of our values and culture and the increase in our taxpayer-funded financial burden for their welfare and social programs.

Years ago the Clinton administration proposed the North American Free Trade Agreement, making it easier for people, commerce, and businesses to wander back and forth over our borders, both the Northern and Southern. But that was before the 9-11-2001 terrorist attacks when America was much more innocent and naïve. Since then, Americans have become keenly aware that not everyone loves and respects America, or at least not the American people, laws, property, or values.

The liberals and Democrats want "Open Borders" but they seem to forget, ignore, or just be ignorant as to what a border represents. As a reminder I'll spell it out: A border (in <u>any</u> country of the world) is a geographically mapped demarcation line indicating the limits of physical land that symbolizes where a specific economic system exists; where an established medium of money and monetary system exists; where a more or less common language is expected to be spoken; where a dominant religion is practiced; where a well-established set of laws is observed; where a certain standard of dress, behavior, and mores is in place; where a military presence is established to protect non-citizens from entering that territory and prevent intrusions from other hostile countries; where commerce and trade are exchanged under certain agreements and treaties; and where a unique shape, color, and design of a flag symbolizes all of these standards and values.

I have no idea how the Democrats get the idea that "open borders" are okay and of no importance. These characteristics and standards apply to every "established" country in the world, allowing that some small parts of the world have yet to formally establish a lasting and stabilized country. And unique to America is a WRITTEN Constitution, well thought out and logically debated by our founders, that clearly establishes our structure of government and its workings, laws, rules, and protections that have been in place for over 230 years. If you get caught illegally crossing the border of almost any country in the world, the punishment is swift and harsh. Again, are Democrats and liberals totally ignorant of the meaning and purposes of borders? Apparently so. Maybe it's a left-brain right-brain thing; women are from Venus, men are from Mars; because surely the differences in thinking and logic between liberals and conservatives are as polarized as they can get.

And when it comes to the Muslims, we see them coming in droves, legally transported, housed, and fed by the taxpaying citizens, but although our INS and other government officials declare it legal, it begs the $64,000 question: Is it just? The Muslims seem to have gotten pretty good at bending and interpreting our laws to suit their needs, but is it just to the rest of the Americans to be displaced by them, like the new developments built for them at taxpayer expense, including a Mosque? Ask the folks in the town of West Virginia what they think is just (it was on a YouTube video). In many ways the Muslims are using our own laws against us when it comes to freedom of religion and free speech. They use our freedoms when it is convenient to use them as they set up restrictions of entry into their neighborhoods and practice and impose Sharia law.

It's interesting that they choose to leave their home country in favor of a relative paradise in America, and then bring their old beliefs and customs with them as they complain in leisure about America. Make no mistake—Muslims came here to destroy America and then take over, otherwise they would be peaceful and assimilate into our culture and obey our laws, or else stay in their home country. Clothing worn to cover the entire body, save the eyes, makes others not only curious, but suspicious. Why cover your face unless you have something to hide? Prejudice against turban wearers comes easy when they are so different from our culture and when they have such a checkered history of violence. Their persistence to wear their traditional garb illustrates their reluctance to assimilate into our melting pot. And the "common man" would likely be willing to overlook these differences were it not for their history of violence.

America is to a point of having way too many inconsistencies of what is legal and what is just. The man on the street knows the difference, and the common taxpayer knows the difference every year on April 15th. Currently about half of the population pays no or very little tax, while the mainstream middle class is paying for much of the rest of society's needs. The lower economic faction criticizes the wealthy without realizing that it's the wealthy, the big corporations, and the "big oil" and "big pharma" that are providing the jobs for everyone, cash flow for home and auto loans, and all the monetary needs that make the world go around. The Democrats shout that it is unjust that the poor are poor, but is it just for the government to abscond the money from those that have gotten financially successful due to their own hard work, creativity, and inventiveness? I say no. I'm certainly not rich by a long shot, but I've never been jealous of anybody that got rich by their own honest means, no matter how rich they are. But now the legal vs. just issue raises its ugly head as we see rich or privileged people like Hillary Clinton and countless other politicians and lawyers literally "getting away with murder" at the expense of others. We've seen the difference between legal vs. just for many years in many forms. Social discrimination between races, discrimination between economic classes, and the disgusting discrimination in our Courts of Law between the common folks and the privileged. The well-known Hollywood set and the wealthy politicians and lawyers come to mind. For instance, O. J. Simpson didn't do it, right? Literally everything pointed to his guilt of murder—his estranged wife, his blood, at her house, in his

Bronco (as it was filmed cruising aimlessly up and down the freeway being followed by the cops, as he tried to decide what to do), with his knife and his get-away money. The world watched the court proceedings and heard it constantly every night on television for months until a slick attorney made the saucy comment about a small sized glove—"If it doesn't fit, you must acquit!" It was totally legal, the trial being conducted in a Court of Law (and a gullible jury instructed by a manipulative Judge bought it), but was it just? Over the past years we've now seen the outcome and behavior of Simpson being set free; he eventually landed in prison for a litany of other civil and criminal offenses, when he should have never been set free in the first place. Again, a clear case of conflict between what is legal and what is just. We clearly have a two-tier legal system—one for the privileged and another for everyone else.

And to this day after literally decades of the shady deaths of many associates of the Clintons, nobody seems to pursue them for all of their questionable dealings, financial frauds, obvious money laundering, dubious foundations, illegal foreign donations, and crimes clearly committed against the government from when Hillary was in office as the Secretary of State. Security breaches, email servers, Benghazi lies, election lies to prevent Trump's election, et cetera, et cetera ad nauseum, and still she and Bill are walking around while Martha Stewart got prison time for what was a relatively small legal infraction compared to all the graft and shenanigans of the Clintons. Again, what's legal vs. what's just.

There are many other examples. Trump wanted to "drain the swamp" but all the Law Enforcement officials in the highest government positions were opposed to his presidency and they almost pulled off a silent coup to overthrow him. I watch the news, and they were almost all Lawyers and Democrats. So ponder it: Legal or just?

We've all heard the saying: Kill a couple of people and you're a criminal, but kill a thousand and you're a hero.

Well, considering the political situation we're in perhaps it's time to start killing our enemies. Remember, Newt Gingrich said it, General Patton said it, and thousands of soldiers have said it, both at home and overseas. And remember, over the years millions, yes, millions, of others have said it by the very Oath that they took to honor and protect our Constitution from _all_ enemies "both foreign and domestic." At the moment the real problem with America is that we haven't had to protect our country militarily from "domestic" enemies since the American Civil War. Over the past 150 years we've forgotten that concept; nowadays we only think our enemies are all from somewhere else around the globe when in fact many enemies are present right under our noses. But the majority of our own people, voters, and politicians are too blind to see it, or else they're in denial that our enemies really do exist right before our faces. We seem to know all about spies hidden under the cover of night and covert operations, but we are deaf and blind to the blatant openness of the enemies presenting themselves to us daily. Muslims. Illegal aliens. Corrupt lawyers, judges, and government officials. Gun controllers. Abortionists.

Just what the hell are we thinking? Well, apparently we aren't (thinking).

Now apply the idea of legal vs. just to the wild idea of Sanctuary Cities and simply ask someone a direct straightforward question: Would you like to see a criminal, druggie, rapist, molester, murderer, or thief move in right next door to you? I bet their answer would be a resounding and vehement NO, regardless of their race, or social, economic, religious, or political conviction (unless they're totally brain dead), and yet we allow the governing bodies of many of our cities and states to invite those same undesirable criminal elements to freely come to our neighborhoods, with the same protections from the laws that we supposedly want for the honest and trustworthy taxpayer next door. On one hand it's ludicrous to have known criminals protected by the same authorities that on the other hand are paying lots of money for law enforcement. No wonder the police are bailing out of their career positions; they're frustrated beyond imagination by the thought of knowing bad criminals and yet being prohibited from apprehending and prosecuting them. These "sanctuary" laws are originated and imposed by officially appointed (and liberal) city councils, so supposedly the concept is legal, but is it just? The liberal mindset is a complicated and hypocritical thing; they love the compassionate touchy-feely position of believing that it's okay for the criminals to live freely and to move freely into someone else's neighborhood, but those same liberals don't want the criminals to live right next door to them. (Check this out with California's Governor and Senators.) Again I ask, it's legal (because some political council says so) but is it just? Liberals don't seem to know how to support their own conflicting political convictions.

And whether it is criminals living in Sanctuary Cities or illegal aliens being supported by money from who knows where, the question remains: who promotes these things? Predominantly liberal local City Councils and State Legislatures for sure. But we also know that Socialist multi-billionaires (and many others with deep pockets) are funding the transportation, shelter, food and clothing for the thousands of non-citizens marching and caravanning north to assault our border, including rebellious organizations like ANTIFA and Black Lives Matter (BLM), and yet nobody seems to say or do anything about it.

I seem to recall a period of our history about a hundred years ago when an FBI Director named J. Edgar Hoover formed committees to investigate Un-American Activities; I also recall the word "seditious acts" being bantered around. So where are those same FBI directors now? Surely somebody sees that Soros is likely funding illegal activities by Clinton and others, and supporting and encouraging the many aliens flooding north to assault our Southern border, and supporting other things that Soros hates, like our anti-gun folks and the freedom to own and use firearms. Ex-President Obama has fallen back to his former occupation as a "Community Organizer" to form his little groups to oppose Trump and literally every move Trump makes to achieve his campaign promises. But I've seen no move to accuse Obama of what is clearly sedition. What we've seen recently as President Trump tries to "drain the swamp," is a vain attempt by officials to ignore the laws and promote seditious acts without retribution. Those same people at the highest echelons of law enforcement (CIA, NSA, FBI) have turned out to be part of the swamp dwellers, and nobody seems to remember J. Edgar Hoover, his interest in un-American activities, or the meaning of the word <u>sedition</u> (Hint: look up the definition of sedition).

Recall the popular saying "Follow the Money" and then think of seditious acts. To me it appears that many of these liberal, socialist, American-hating billionaires are the Charles Manson's of the financial world; they are wantonly and openly

51

killing America (or trying). How hypocritical of them to have profited greatly from the American systems and freedoms, and then turn around to bite the hand that has fed them. What they're doing is (apparently?) legal, but is it just? All I see is unjust "seditious acts" and they need to be held accountable.

Then comes the issue of universal healthcare. For all? It's nowhere to be seen or even hinted at in the U.S. Constitution. First, it would be unimaginably expensive and would totally break the budget of a government already $30+ Trillion in debt, and second, why would we even dream of funding universal healthcare (for Americans AND illegal aliens!) while we give—yes, outright GIVE—millions and billions of dollars of "Foreign Aid" to countries all over the world, many of which hate our guts. Yep, our government giving Foreign Aid to countries that hate our country, our politics, and our people is legal, but is it just to many of our own citizens that (apparently) need healthcare, but we can't afford providing their healthcare because the U.S. is already $30 Trillion in debt? But then we still give out "foreign aid" by the bucketsful. Foreign aid: It's legal, but it's hardly just to be giving money to countries that totally oppose our very own systems and philosophies of government, and the values dear to most of the taxpayers of America. I'm fiercely patriotic, but some of the things that America does are downright stupid.

> *"Youth ages, immaturity is outgrown, ignorance can be educated, and drunkenness sobered, but stupid lasts forever."* — Aristophanes 446-386 B.C.

Welcome to big government, where the left hand doesn't know what the right hand is doing, and the Democrats keep wanting to increase the bulk of our government with policies that are just plain stupid, and massive costs that are unsustainable.

So let's touch on Gun Control, a real "hot button" for liberals. They think guns kill, when any sane and experienced gun owner can see that deaths are caused by PEOPLE that misuse guns. Yes, people kill people, by many means, but guns are only inanimate tools and only intentionally kill others when there is a miscreant holding on to the gun. And make no mistake, the ownership of guns in the hands of honest people is the only thing that stands in the way of an eventual take-over by the Democrats and Socialists.

Now consider the current state of world affairs. As stated clearly in the previous pages, America is unmistakably under assault—from illegal aliens, from as far south of our border as South America, and from Muslims that have openly vowed to kill us all or subdue us, and they've stated (and have pretty well proven) that they won't stop their Jihad until we are all dead or living under their Sharia Laws. And internally we're on the brink of Civil War between our own citizens that are violently and openly opposed to the Constitution and conservatism.

From Wikipedia:

Molon Labe (mo-lone lah-veh)
"Two little words. With these two words, two concepts were verbalized that have lived for nearly two and a half Millennia. They signify and characterize both the heart of the Warrior, and the indomitable spirit of mankind.

"In 480 B.C. the forces of the Persian Empire under King Xerxes, numbering, according to Herodotus, two million men, bridged the Hellespont and marched in their myriads to invade and enslave Greece.

"After days of fighting and having killed countless numbers of Xerxes' elite troops, they were finally overrun after being betrayed by a traitor who showed the enemy another pass behind the defenders. King Leonidas, his Spartans and their Thespian allies died to the last man. Xerxes marched on and destroyed Athens. The standard of valor set by this sacrifice inspired the Greeks to rally and, in that fall and spring, defeat the Persians at Salamis and Plataea and preserve the beginnings of Western democracy and freedom from perishing in the cradle.

"Two memorials remain today at Thermopylae. Upon the modern one, called the Leonidas Monument in honor of the Spartan king who fell there, is engraved on a marble slab is his response to Xerxes' demand that the Spartans lay down their arms. Leonidas' reply was two words: Molon Labe (or variously translated) 'Come and get them.'

"The second monument is a plaque dedicated to those heroes at the site. It reads: 'Go tell the Spartans, travelers passing by, that here, obedient to their laws we lie.'

"The point of this true story is when anybody demands you to give up your arms, tell them 'MOLON LABE.'" These words live on today as the most notable quote in military history. And so began the classic example of courage and valor in its dismissal of overwhelming superiority of numbers, wherein the heart and

spirit of brave men overcame insuperable odds. We have adopted this defiant utterance as a battle cry in our war against oppression because it says so clearly and simply towards those who would take our arms. It signifies our determination to not strike the first blow, but also to not stand mute and allow our loved ones, and all that we believe in and stand for, to be trampled by men who would deprive us of our God-given—or natural, if you will—rights, just to suit their own ends."

And Democrats or the government want to disarm Americans?! Do they really think that TRULY patriotic Americans will surrender their firearms anytime, or especially at a time when we're being assaulted at our borders, by Muslims that have vowed to kill us, and by anarchists and Liberals that want to convert Capitalism to Socialism?

Don't hold your breath. ("...*from my cold, dead hands!*" – Charlton Heston)

The Second Amendment should have been the First, as the ownership of guns is the first line of defense from tyranny. With an armed citizenry, the leftists have a harder time of taking over the country, but they can do it slowly by other seditious and subversive ways. Like infiltrating our educational system and controlling what we read or see in the news and on social media via the internet. We are seeing the power of the social media as we speak, with the large companies monitoring written content and keeping track of who says what in their communications. The large media monopolies have even gone so far as to censure many of their own subscribers due to the content of their political comments. We even see that some publishing companies are picking and choosing who can get their books published by their companies—note that Republican Missouri Senator Josh Hawley was recently denied publication by a large and popular book company that had previously indicated that they would publish his book. A case of not-so-subtle censuring of Free Speech if you ask me.

Gun control. Thought control. Control of communications. Censorship of certain ideas and books. Nazi Germany? China or Russia? Nope—in America. As we speak.

Constitutional Considerations

Since the Constitution was enacted there have been many attempts to "fine tune" it to suit the "modern" conventions, attitudes, and emergence of technologies and science. But it is becoming increasingly clear that at least some changes need to be made in the Constitution due to the fact that our Founding Fathers couldn't have possibly anticipated the world 230 years in the future. They did a very good job at forming our Constitution then, but now…?

Term Limits

The Founders intended to have representatives serve for a short term in government and then go back to their regular jobs and businesses, but we now have "professional" politicians that get into House and Senate seats early in their life and stay there for decades before they either retire or die in office. We all know who they are: Feinstein 60 years; Schumer 45 years; Maxine

Waters 47 years; Joe Biden 51 years; Nancy Pelosi 33 years; Patrick Leahy 54 years. All Democrats. Any long-term Republicans? Sure, but they aren't trying to tear down the system like the Democrats are. Term limits are imposed on the Office of the President, so why aren't there limits on Senators, Congressmen, and yes, even the Justices of the Supreme Court? These politicians wouldn't be in ANY position if the VOTERS didn't put them there, but we've seen some pretty ignorant and naïve voters interviewed on the street that are totally irresponsible when it comes to knowledge of modern politics or American or world history. This reflects a dismal failure of our Educational System that has severely decayed over the past several generations; young people have not adequately been taught ethics, morals, civics, religion, history, or the Constitution.

> *"In questions of power, then, let not more be heard of confidence in man, but bind him down from mischief by the chains of the Constitution."* –Thomas Jefferson

The 17th Amendment now gives the general voters the right to select Senators, when the Founding Fathers originally intended that Senators be selected by their learned and experienced peers as stated in Article 1, Sec. 3 of the Constitution. These days anyone off the street could be elected to this important position, which seems wrong to this writer.

BALANCED BUDGET

"I, however, place **economy** *among the first and most important republican virtues, and public debt as the greatest of dangers to be feared. To preserve our independence, we must not let our rulers load us* **with perpetual debt.** *I am for a government rigorously frugal and simple."* –Thomas Jefferson

Our current massive national budget is extremely complex to calculate, but for about the first century our government tried diligently to pay its debts and tried not to carry over debts to the following generation. On January 8, 1835, President Andrew Jackson paid off the entire national debt, the only time in U.S. history that has been accomplished. In 1836 debt began again (the debt on January 1, 1836, was $37,000). Another sharp increase in the debt occurred as a result of the Civil War. The debt was just $65 million in 1860, but passed $1 billion in 1863 and reached $2.7 billion by the end of the war. During the following 47 years, there were 36 surpluses and 11 deficits. During this period 55% of the national debt was paid off.

Our Founding Fathers felt it to be immoral and unethical to spend large sums of money and then leave the debt to the following generations; they took their fiscal responsibilities seriously. That we are now in debt to the tune of about $30 TRILLION is unconscionable, and much of that debt is held by the Chinese. Somehow we need to have a method in our Constitution that prevents our "leaders" from spending money that the taxpayers can't afford. Remember, there is no such thing as "Government Money." It ALL comes from the pockets of the hardworking American taxpayers via the collection by the IRS and distribution by Congress.

Our founders warned against the "cradle to grave" welfare state, confiscatory taxation, and deficit spending. Thomas Jefferson said it was immoral for one generation to pass on the results of its extravagance in the form of debts to the next generation, but considering our current unfathomable national debt, our founding fathers and Jefferson must be absolutely spinning in their graves.

Our Second Amendment

The Constitutional PROTECTION for our right to bear arms is in the foundational document of the basic laws and rights for the citizens of the USA. For 200 years our citizens carried their firearms pretty much without issues except for local Sheriffs presumably like Wyatt Earp that told the cowboys headed for the bar to "check their weapons" (which if true was one of the early infringements on the Second Amendment protections). But in the past few decades, the various States have started doing their own version of gun control, most of which are clearly unconstitutional and yet the Federal legislatures and the Supreme Court seem reluctant to say anything about it. In many states it's almost impossible to get a firearm, even if you're a resident of that state. The stacks of paperwork and the required exorbitant fees make it a de facto ban on guns, especially handguns, and the most strident offenders are the Democrat-dominated states like NY, NJ, IL, and CA. Perhaps it's time to reiterate the unique freedom we enjoy in the United States of being able to have an armed citizenry, one that was purposely intended to hold at bay a potential future tyrannical government. And these days, that potential reality might be needed if voters put into office some of the current antigun legislators. Right now the gun laws for Open Carry and Concealed Carry vary from state to state, and the citizen traveling across state lines is faced with a blizzard of laws that are nearly impossible to keep up with or comply with.

During periods of national emergencies, citizens look to firearms for a measure of comfort for personal protection. In America, there are an estimated 393 million firearms in the possession of 326 million American civilians (Wikipedia: Global Small Arms Survey 2017). And as a result of the 2020 COVID-19 pandemic and the uncertainty of the outcome of the 2020 National Elections, the number of _new_ (first-time) gun buyers in 2020 was about 5 million, with the total of guns bought in 2020 well over 12 million from just January through July. The year 2020 will doubtless set a record for gun sales in America (NRA—November 2020).

So for all the gun owners in America, we need a NATIONAL policy, consistent throughout all states, that clearly defines the Constitutional protections afforded by the Second Amendment, and clearly honors the reciprocity between states for allowing citizens to carry their arms concealed. The Constitutional 2nd Amendment is a FEDERAL law, a "law of the land"; how it got to be applied and perverted inconsistently throughout the individual States is a mystery to Patriotic law abiding Americans. There should be no hesitation of the honest law-abiding citizen to have a firearm and yet be faced with fines, court appearances, or jail time for having a gun found in his car during a routine traffic stop by the police, regardless of the state through which he happens to be traveling. In addition, by extension, there needs to be a clear prohibition on local town, city, and county councils, governors, and mayors to override these National policies. We certainly don't need more "gun laws" or "gun-free zones" that are supposed to make us all safer; what we need is to simply enforce equally, equitably, and fairly the hundreds of gun laws already on the books, and make those laws <u>consistent</u> throughout the country—for every State, County, and City—at the Federal level. The inconsistency of Constitutional gun laws and their enforcement is another issue that tends to divide America.

SECURE OUR BORDERS

That we should secure our borders to help prevent intrusions by illegal aliens was supported by every politician from Clinton to Obama until President Donald Trump came into office. Suddenly those same Democrats changed their tune simply because they hated Trump and wanted to see him fail at every suggestion he made. The Democrats said that building a border wall was too expensive and not humanitarian, while at the same time we were inundated by Mexicans and others from Central America, and OTMs (Other Than Mexicans) of whom we had no idea of who they are, where they're from, or their intensions for harming us.

Common sense tells us we need to know who comes and goes in America, especially in light of the disasters that occurred on Sept. 11, 2001.

As an extension of the issue of border security, we need to eliminate the nonsensical Lottery for 55,000 aliens that can come to America simply because they were fortunate enough to have their name pulled from a hat. Those foreigners are required only to have a certain minimum of skills and work experience. Again, are we just plain stupid or what?

It's time America began taking only the best of people that have the potential to become productive and patriotic citizens, and not those that have the prospect to end up on the roles as welfare recipients.

ENGLISH AS OUR NATIONAL LANGUAGE

Although there are many foreign languages spoken and used consistently by American citizens, by convention (and majority) our traditional national language is obviously English. However, America should establish English as the _Official National Language_ for business, commerce, and schools. Why? Because being able to clearly communicate with each other—every citizen to every other citizen—is about the only "glue" that keeps us together as a culture and a Nation. Our very diverse culture has many languages, religions, manners of dress, races, and national origins, and certain commonalities are vital. English is one of those few but vital commonalities; there are innate suspicions between people that can't understand each other when attempting to converse.

Another commonality we should all have is the use of a consistent currency and coinage. I believe there are small enclaves in America that use other means of currency for trade, like bartering, computer digital "money," and other city and village tokens. A "standard" of value makes fair trade truly <u>Fair</u> trade, and again, acts as a common "glue" that keeps us on a financial par of understanding with each other.

PRESERVING OUR HISTORY

The desecration of any of our Public statues, monuments, symbols, and structures should be illegal and should carry appropriate penalties. Freedom of expression doesn't have to be destructive and perverted as a means for self-expression, and just because someone doesn't agree with or like our history doesn't change that history. These symbols aren't meant to be torn down, they're meant to be studied and LEARNED from!

NATIONAL STANDARDS FOR PUBLIC SCHOOLS

"A well instructed people alone can be permanently a free people." –James Madison

America needs to set higher—and enforceable—standards for high school graduation, regardless of geographic location, city, or state. We've all heard of instances of kids graduating that can hardly read, write, or do basic math. Graduation should not be granted for those that cannot academically prove that they are ready to advance to the next grade, regardless of their age or what grade they're in. Student advancement should not be just for the pleasure of the teachers and administrators or to make a student "feel good" that he graduated. And for the public educational school system to rely on good statistics simply to get good funding is missing the point of being a SCHOOL.

Also, there should be a change in which subjects should be mandatory vs. electives, such as Constitution, ethics, history, religion, and civics. This writer strongly believes that the civil unrest of our modern-day stems from the fact that fewer and fewer students have the very basics of what makes America function. Some voting-age young people can't even tell the name of our first U.S. president, the names of our founding fathers, or dates of our Civil War and why or where the war was fought.

LEGAL SYSTEM REFORM

In some areas of our legal system, JUSTICE should be more consistent throughout our country. In particular, the death penalty, gun laws, and abortion.

For instance, for being convicted of unspeakable, vicious, violent, repeated, unforgivable, and unrepentant crime, some criminals are sentenced to the death penalty and some are sentenced to imprisonment. Our states vary as to the penalty for the very same crime; some states allow the death penalty and some do not. And some that DO allow the death penalty also allow legal appeals that go on for years and even decades. We might recognize the "quick and speedy trial" part of our Constitution, but this flies in the face of justice for those vicious criminals sentenced to death, and justice for the victims and their families. Prolonged indecision might even be considered cruel and unusual punishment for some people. This begs the question of what is legal versus what it just.

So let me pose the question:

On one hand, how can many states <u>deny</u> the death penalty for these heinous criminals while on the other hand <u>allow</u> the killing of <u>millions</u> of totally innocent and perfectly normal babies, many of which are killed at the moment of birth, or even AFTER the birth by simple, intentional neglect of care?

I'll wait for your answer—as long as it takes….Again, legal vs. just?

Our governors, legislators, Congress, and Supreme Court should blush at the question posed.

Shame on Americans, shame on the Federal government, and shame *especially* on our Supreme Court for allowing abortions and allowing the inconsistency of the application of the death penalty. Talk about a conflict of philosophies…!

Consider that there are generally several security levels for prisons—Minimum security, Low, Medium, and High security, and the most secure that is labeled as Maximum or "Supermax" Prisons for those criminals that pose the extremely highest risk for violence and public safety and have ZERO hope of ever being rehabilitated or let loose. Again let me pose the question: If these criminals are so dangerous and irredeemable, why would the general public want to sustain them in prisons in their peaceful neighborhoods and communities? I've heard the argument that it costs more to execute a prisoner than to hold the criminal in prison for the rest of his life. But I argue that the high cost of execution is only because of lawyers and the prolonged legal wrangling, not the cost of the execution. A rope, a bullet, or electrocution can't possibly cost very much *if carried out efficiently and expeditiously*. The huge cost to build and maintain a brick-and-mortar maximum security structure along with its ongoing utility costs, the cost of 24/7/365 prison guards and administration (and their ongoing retirement costs), the cost of food and medical care, and other endless visible and hidden costs seems undoubtedly MORE than the expeditious cost of execution if we could find a way to lessen the involvement of our lawyers and courts. These unspeakable criminals are simply considered throwaways and should be, well, thrown away—executed—instead of being a cost and safety risk for the taxpaying public. But killing babies is still okay.... And don't pervert the abortion argument; I'm talking about perfectly normal, viable babies, in the womb from the moment of conception, not the special cases that involve genetic problems, risk to the mother, etc. Abortion for convenience is simply murder. Period. But we let our most dangerous criminals get away with murder every day, legally by endless appeals, for years, in prisons. So tell me, *please*, where's the justice?

WELFARE REFORM

Too many people that could work WON'T work because it isn't worth their time and energy. Plus, there are costs associated with working, like bus fare or car ownership costs and maintenance, clothes, outside childcare, and purchasing your own tools or other work supplies, to say nothing about the income taxes and social security tax that will be deducted out of your weekly paycheck.

The solution is for the States and Federal government to set the worker minimum wage <u>high</u> enough to give people the incentive to work, while setting the welfare entitlement <u>so low</u> that it is at the level of bare minimum subsistence for those physically and mentally able to work. Basically, the gap between minimum wages and welfare pay needs to be much wider.

The problem now is that too many people on welfare are capable of working, but the deadbeats are not being screened well enough to weed them out. Too many people are abusing the welfare system and getting away with it.

Welfare is certainly well justified for many of our more unfortunate citizens that can't work due to conditions beyond their control, such as poor health, physical and mental birth defects, old age, military disablement, serious car wrecks and work accidents, etc. I know—my brother was in that category all his life.

A wealthy and compassionate society should take care of the genuinely needy, but giving away our taxpayer money to those not in need is an abuse of our system. A rich nation should afford a reasonable standard of living for the genuinely needy, and weed out the freeloaders.

TREASONOUS AND SEDITIOUS ACTIVITY

Our country is now seeing more civil unrest than since the Civil War. Vietnam protests in the '60s, race protests over integration in schools, and riots in the Watts district of Los Angeles weren't as bad as the civil unrest that we are seeing right now, and the rioting is rampant in many large cities all across the country.

And there is a reason.

Rich left wingers are funding (and Obama is organizing) the puppets that are being used as instruments for destroying America.

This anti-American movement started seriously during the Clinton Administration when "politically correct" language began. The Obama Administration wanted to "basically transform America" (his speech) and put in place Hillary Clinton and John Kerry as Secretaries of State that allowed Middle East factions to dominate the populations of non-Muslims and attack our American embassies, bomb our Naval ships and military Marine barracks, and allow immigration to the U.S. of terrorists that would eventually pull off the most destructive attack yet on September 11, 2001, when airliners were used as bombs in New York City, the Pentagon in Washington, D.C., and in Pennsylvania.

Again, the peaceful Tea Party protesters had their signs exactly accurate: OBAMA—**O**ne **B**ig **A**ss **M**istake **A**merica!

And amazingly, during the second term of Obama's Presidency, Obama quietly began organizing leftist resistance groups to oppose any future Conservative politicians or groups. Originally named OFA (Organization For America), the name soon morphed into Organization For Action and the organization began recruiting volunteers to form even more groups that subscribed to "progressive" political philosophies. These groups included Planned Parenthood, MoveOn, the ACLU, Sierra Club, SEIU, NAACP, the International Brotherhood of

Electrical Workers (IBEW), Common Sense, Sunrise Movement, League of Women Voters, National Organization of Women (NOW), and at least a dozen others.

From 2013 to 2018 the OFA had over 62,000 people that were trained on skills needed to "make an impact" and gathered over 7,570,000 online "action-takers" that could respond quickly to any issue that arose that could be pertinent to their cause. By 2018 OFA had organized 154 active chapters from coast to coast, and held well over 30,000 grassroots events across all 50 states. Nearly every modern-day President has retired after leaving office or gone peacefully back to his home state, but not Obama. He stayed in Washington, D.C., to linger around and stink up the place for the incoming Conservative President Trump. The seditious activities of the many political action groups and organizations now in play have Obama's fingerprints all over them, and in my opinion, every one of these "progressive" organizations should be investigated for violations of the Racketeer Influenced and Corrupt Organizations Act and treasonous and seditious activity.

OFA kicked into high gear the instant it became apparent that Donald Trump was a serious contender for the Republican Party. Trump was elected President just when the silent coup by the Democrats was attempted, which was exposed and failed dismally. Funding for the corrupt law enforcement agency heads was undoubtedly arranged, organized, and funded by Democrats in high places, along with rich Socialist billionaires that hated Trump to the point that they were willing to destroy the country in order to destroy him. These people that dominated the House attempted to impeach the President, and they failed. These people are clearly guilty of trying to overthrow a valid election of President Trump, and it astonishes millions of citizens as to why these seditious and treasonous people aren't facing the death penalty. In the good old days they would be! Former FBI Director J. Edgar Hoover would have seen to it, and hanging or imprisonment wouldn't have taken decades to accomplish like it does now. Where have all the GOOD GUYS gone? Where have the honest citizens gone that would shout for justice for America's treasonous enemies? Why are Hillary Clinton and Barrack Obama still walking around free? Americans are hungry for true justice, all while ANTIFA and BLM riots and burns down buildings all across America.

> *"We in America do not have government by the majority—we have government by the majority <u>who participate</u>...All tyranny needs to gain a foothold is for people of good conscience to remain silent."*
>
> —Thomas Jefferson

Patriotic American Protesting

So now the massive fraudulent voting from the Democrats has resulted in the election of Joe Biden, an entrenched bureaucrat of 50 years who has produced no significant legislation, along with his appointed Vice President that is an openly admitted avowed Socialist. The Conservatives are finally fed up with the fraud, with the incompetence of the voting system, and the fraudulent prospect of an incompetent President. Virtually ALL the public and legal complaints about the vote have been from the Republicans due to the totally lopsided results of the 2020 Presidential elections. Virtually NO complaints about the vote results or the vote process, have been from the Democrats. Common sense would say that the noise from the Republicans is justified, while the Democrats stand quiet with a smirk on their face with no effective (yet) legal repercussions.

Why is the reaction so one sided? Because the Republicans, by their very nature, are morally honest, conservative in their behavior, and knowledgeable and respectful of the Constitution, and they observe the rule of law. But the Democrats by their very nature are liars, radical in their behavior (BLM or ANTIFA—anyone?), and disrespectful of the Constitution (2nd Amendment attacks for a start). And Democrats are willing to bend whatever rules are necessary in order to win. That is the *strength* of the Democrats, while respect for law is the *weakness* of the Republicans. Hence, when corruption occurs, fraudulent voting occurs, disruptive protesting occurs, or unconstitutional bending of the rules occurs, the Democrats win and the Conservatives lose. While the Democrats are politically ruthless, the Republicans are just too damned nice.

This discontent by the Conservatives has been building like a pressure cooker for decades. Refer to the Prologue of this writing and note that ALL the protesting by the quickly formed Tea Party against Obama was peaceful. Note that ALL the "questionable" voting results for decades was peacefully tolerated by the Conservatives for the agonizing years of the Clinton and Obama administrations, and the blatant misconduct of Hillary Clinton, John Kerry, and all the players of the attempted coup of the Trump administration, perpetrated by the highest officials of the CIA, FBI, NSA, and the corrupt members of the House of Representatives that had built a phony case about Russian corruption in order to impeach Trump.

Now, in January of 2020, we were finally seeing predictable backlash and pushback from the Conservatives over the outcome of the recounts of the Georgia Senate elections, and the proven fraudulent elections that resulted in Wisconsin, Pennsylvania, Arizona, Michigan, Nevada, and Georgia. For the first time in modern history, the thousands of Patriotic, peaceful, flag-waving Conservatives were trying to make their voices heard by gathering in the D.C. mall, while a few radicals physically swarmed the Capitol building during the session of Congress that was dealing with the results and processing of the Electoral College. Predictably, the police were trying to do their job, while a few BLM/ANTIFA members infiltrated the peaceful protesters to make trouble so to make the Trump patriots look bad. We already knew that Soros, Clinton, Obama, and others with deep pockets would fund the hell raisers and do anything to make Trump and his supporters look bad. And the mainstream media fell for it and reported all things bad instead of accepting the facts of the fraudulent voting.

I find it remarkable that all the gays fill the D.C. mall to protest, and their gay rights get recognized; all the blacks fill the D.C. mall to protest and their race rights get recognized; all the women fill the D.C. mall and their women's rights get recognized. But when all the PATRIOTS (which include ALL the other above groups) fill the mall, <u>most that are proudly waving AMERICAN FLAGS</u>, they get castigated, criticized by the media, and beat up by the police! Welcome to the new world where we are seeing America slide inexorably into Socialism. And make no mistake—the rest of the world is watching the

USA very closely. Will we remain the last refuge in the world for freedom or not?

This was a tipping point in our history when we started seeing the Republicans and Conservatives demanding that our government "do the right thing" and rightfully install Trump to the White House for his second term. The cause and the evidence was overwhelming, and Trump truly won. Period. If the Democrats could win in this current battle, this country would be slated to slide into socialism. If the Trump conservatives would win, we would hopefully have a massive reform of our voting system that would help assure more honest elections, now and in the future. It takes courage to upset the apple cart, but there were a number of Republicans that weren't reluctant to contest the status quo, so they voted against Trump and sealed the fate for denying Trump a second term. Civil war is becoming a real possibility, and if it first occurs BY the Conservatives it will be BECAUSE of the Democrats. Respectful people can only take so much, and doing nothing is no longer an option. Those days might be coming to an end.

Again, all it takes for evil to occur is for good people to do nothing. I revere and support the police, but when they beat up on the patriots waving flags, they're beating up the wrong people. Maybe it's time for them to start taking sides.

VETTING AND VOTING

Another indication that "the other side" is winning is the selection of the candidates for elected office, especially the most important high offices. When Obama came on the scene there was fevered activity to find out just who he was, and the public quickly found that all his records had been sequestered. Not only were his birth records kept secret, but also his school and college records, and all other records that could show his origin of birth and history of his travel, such as passports. Since Obama is now out of office, emails and other videos of him speaking have clandestinely been produced that show him admitting that he was born in Kenya. His self-admitted profession as a Muslim runs true to what we saw when he went on his world tour shortly after his inauguration—bowing to Imams, having no American flags on the stages when he presented speeches, and so on. During one of his campaign speeches he bragged that he had campaigned in all 57 states. The man obviously had a dismal knowledge of America and its history. And it begs the question: If many people in the general public knew about him, why didn't the Democrats know it? The higher Democrat party members would have HAD to know it, but chose to let him pass as legitimately being constitutionally eligible to be seated into the Office of President, regardless of what the rules are in the Constitution. I can't understand why NOBODY in the FBI, CIA, NSA or any other intelligence agency caught this vital flaw, or if they did, why they ignored it. It smelled and smacked of corruption, mainly from Democrat sympathizers whether they were high in the food chain or well embedded bureaucrats. (Of course we now know that the problem was the bias of the highest Obama-appointed officials in those agencies.)

Therefore, I believe it should be incumbent on the Supreme Court to verify the eligibility of all House, Senate, and

Presidential candidates prior to their campaigning. We've proven that at least one party promoting their candidate isn't to be trusted. It goes without saying that there is a vital need for election reform; simply too many deceased people are voting from the grave as well as too many non-citizens. The 2020 elections were an absolute fiasco with obvious voter fraud and stuffing of ballot boxes, variations in state-to-state voting and documentation processes, and voting deadline violations.

National Voting Reform

Again, our Founding Fathers couldn't have possibly foreseen the variety of ways that the various states would address (or pervert or bias) our voting process when it came to how the Electoral College would work.

Granted, the individual States have (and probably should have) the right to structure their own process for electing their own state level officials as they see fit, according to their demographics, geography, size, predominant culture, tax structure, traffic laws, natural resources, trade opportunities, time zones, etc., making each state out of the 50 unique in their approach to issues within the boundaries of their State. Obviously, Alaska, Hawaii, California, Wyoming, and New York are all as different from each other as day and night. But to this writer it only makes sense that for *NATIONAL* elections the voting process <u>should be the same for every State</u>. After all, our elected President is the <u>ONE</u>, National, **U.S.** President, equally, for ALL States.

Therefore, this author believes that the PROCESS for voting should be consistent throughout each and every state for NATIONAL elections. At the moment, the state-to-state voting processes are a scrambled mess, with no consistencies in time, places, laws, rules, processes, considerations of time zones, or security of public knowledge as the votes are counted and processed. Presently, mail-in ballots, ballot harvesting, third-person delivery, signature verification, delivery dates, US Postal Service involvement, etc., are inconsistent and totally unmanaged, uncontrollable, and unverifiable.

An interesting phenomena of the public is the "follow the herd" mentality of voting for whoever is ahead in the polls, because nobody wants to vote for a loser. So consider that the voters in Alaska and Hawaii are watching the outcome on television or internet as the day passes. Due to the vast time-zone differences across the total of America, they see and hear information hours before the end of the national voting, and they make up their minds because of the influence of previous voters and the news blasts from the MSM as the counting unfolds. In my opinion, there should be a political-news blackout until ALL the votes across the country are decided, at least for 24 hours, to allow for unbiased voters to decide for themselves as to how they should vote, without the influence of others or the wildly unpredictable mainstream media. Simply put, the voters have NO confidence in the integrity of their vote, due to the inconsistencies state-to-state of how the ballots are handled, counted, and processed. The discovery of trash bags of ballots found in dumpsters and back alleys weeks after the elections is not the way to handle the most important elections in our country. And if you live in the farthest western time zones, why even vote if you can see that the results are already decided by the vast bulk of the previous voters five or six hours ahead of them?

And let's make it perfectly clear: The problem is NOT because of the Electoral College. The problem is at the *State level* because the votes for the Electoral College are NOT handled by all the States *consistently*.

For instance in some States, if 51% of the people in a particular State vote for the Democrat Presidential candidate and the other 49% vote for the Republican, *ALL* the State Electoral votes go the Electoral college as Democrat. To be fair, only 51% should go to the Democrat candidate, not 100%. The votes should be proportional to the Electoral College the same as the voters indicated at the State level. Nation Wide. It's only fair to the minority that at least their votes meant something; with the current process the minority votes might as well be tossed in the trash when it comes to National elections. And although in America at the City, County, and State levels, where 51% majority might win by only one percent, it still leaves 49% of the voters unhappy about the outcome. With a proportional vote at the *Federal* level, that 49% have a much better prospect of their voices being heard when it comes time to count votes at the Electoral College. To me, this issue seems to fit the justification for a Constitutional Convention of States.

Just to touch on the fraudulent voting that has taken place in the past few decades, let's look at the statistics of the 2020 elections that have led the Trump administration to legally contest the validity of the voting system clear to the top level of our government lawyers—the Supreme Court.

(The below is from several news and internet sources, but the writer is unknown to this author.)

TO ALL AMERICANS WHO QUESTION THE INTEGRITY OF THE ELECTION

CPAs are the most trusted professionals in America and are trained to "audit" companies' financials as to whether they are fairly stated. As a part of these audits we do statistical sampling and look for statistical abnormalities. Put on your auditor hat and consider these things and tell me if you would put your career on the line and sign off saying this election fairly represents the results of the vote.

- At midnight on election night electoral map vote counts had Trump winning in a landslide with over 300 electoral votes.

- At 6 A.M. a dump in Michigan gave Biden 141,258 votes and Trump 5,968.

- At 3 A.M. a dump in Wisconsin gave Biden 143,379 and Trump 25,163.

- At 1 A.M. a dump in Georgia gave Biden 136,155 votes and 29,115 to Trump.

- These dumps only happened in key swing states where Trump previously held leads. They did not happen in Democrat-strong or Republican-strong states and the polling places that were closed without oversight.

- Election graphs after these dumps had vertical spikes which are virtually impossible and never happened before.

- The vote spikes totals in these states matched almost exactly the margins that Biden needed to win.

- 74 million people voted for Trump in 2020 which is 11m more than 2016. Statistically no president in history has ever lost reelection when he expanded his voter base.

- Trump grew his base among black voters by 50%.

- Biden received 80m votes when Obama only received 69m in 2008 when he was statistically one of the highest rated presidents among Democrats in modern history.

- Biden won a RECORD low of only 17% of counties in the entire country.

- Trump won 18 of the 19 counties that historically predict the winner. Statistically a loss is next to impossible.

- Biden would be the first president in 60 years to lose both Florida and Ohio and still win.

- Biden massively under-performed Hillary Clinton except in a few "key" counties, yet he won and Hillary lost.

- Biden massively under-performed Hillary in every major metro area around the country except Milwaukee, Detroit, Atlanta, and Philadelphia, yet he won and she lost (all the areas where vote dumps happened when polls where closed).

- Biden won despite Democrat losses nationwide: Republicans appear to have won all 27 "toss up seats" in local elections, gained significant seats in the House and should have maintained control of the Senate. So Republicans went and voted for their local seats but against the most popular Republican president in modern history—Trump got 94% of primary vote—no incumbent who received 75% of primary vote has ever *lost* reelection.

  A record 18m voters showed up to support Trump in the primary which is more than any president in history. Previous record was Clinton with 9m.

- Biden didn't campaign, he didn't inspire, and could barely speak regularly, forgetting words or seemingly making up words.

And the thinking public is supposed to believe that Trump lost this election FAIRLY?

Be sure to see the several embedded links in the *DeepCapture* news source, written by Patrick Byrne, former CEO of the furniture company Overstock, that give a convincing technical analysis of the November 2020 election results. Watch especially the 21-minute video of an interview of Seth Keshel, an Army Captain that has a background in military intelligence, as he is interviewed by Doug Wade of the *DeepCapture* news (htpps://youtu.be/xXMW9VNMPT4).

More *indisputable* proof can be seen in the same *DeepCapture* news video by mathematician Edward Soloman entitled *Geometric Proof For Georgia* that describes in great detail the workings of the algorithms of the voting machines that were manipulated to give the Georgia win to Biden. He also gives a similar analysis of the precincts of Philadelphia where the ballots were "flipped" to favor Biden when there was an interruption in the vote counting during the wee hours of election night. He discusses "shenanigans" of the voting machines that are capable of being manipulated, and he shows vote ratios of Biden:Trump in precincts that are the same, precinct after precinct after precinct. Exact ratios are highly unlikely and statistically nearly impossible, especially when the voting history of the precincts is examined.

From another article, on March 10, 2021, Petr Svab wrote for the *Epoch Times* online news service that "more than 90,000 ballots mailed to registered voters in Nevada's largest county were returned undeliverable, according to an analysis of election data by a conservative legal group." (That would be Clark County which is basically Las Vegas and the entire surrounding area, the largest metropolitan area in the otherwise mostly rural Nevada.) "More than 450,000 voters cast their votes through the mail-in ballots. But more than 92,000 ballots were returned by the postal service as undeliverable, according to the Public Interest Legal Foundation's (PILF) March 10 research brief."

To put this in perspective the article further states "the entire state of Nevada reported only 5,863 mail ballots returned undeliverable in the 2012, 2014, 2016, and 2018 General Elections COMBINED" (emphasis added) referring to the U.S. Election Assistance Commission surveys."

So compare four different years of General Elections totaling 5,863 undeliverable returned ballots, to 92,000 ballots returned by just ONE COUNTY in just ONE ELECTION! Small wonder that Trump justifiably squawked about the questionable integrity of the voting system.

So again, did Biden win Georgia fairly? Did he win Michigan fairly? Wisconsin? Florida and Ohio? Of course he won Nevada fairly—by 92,000 undeliverable votes from just one county alone....

The election system is broken.

And then we see the unconstitutional involvement of the various Governors and Attorneys General telling the vote counters what they can and can't do to verify and certify "honest" votes, when it is addressed by the Constitution as to certain processes and certifications. The 2020 elections were a joke, which prompted massive protests in the Washington, D.C., mall in the first week of January 2021, and left Georgia voters with the task of recounting and having to conduct a second vote for the Governorship.

The two Georgia Democrat candidate choices for the Senate were either an abject radical Socialist preacher, or a young man that had ZERO significant leadership or government experience or work history.

Again, Thank You for the Seventeenth Amendment of 1913 that allows the <u>election</u> of Senators from any common "man on the street" in their individual states "...elected by the *people* thereof." The *original* Constitutional election of Senators as per Article I, Section 3, was for two Senators from each state to be "*chosen by the LEGISLATURE.*" In other words the Senators were "appointed" to the Senate by their learned peers, associates, and colleges that knew them and knew that they had talents, were experienced in government, and had good reputations. Compare that metric with some of the Senators currently being chosen by the Democrat party. It's laughable if not outright stupid and dangerous to place incompetent people in positions of power and authority. And remember, only stupid voters would put in office stupid politicians. Remember the grilling of a Navy Admiral that was asked by a Democrat if the construction of a Navy base on Guam would cause the island to "tip over" into the sea? To the credit of the Admiral, he kept a straight face and was gracious enough not to make the questioner look like an ass. I saw it live, personally, on TV, and not just once but several other times when the news broadcasters couldn't believe the stupidity. This is the kind of people our citizens are voting into office, thanks to our failed Public School system.

UNIONS IN PUBLIC SERVICE

There should be a ban on having Unions in any and all Public service organizations. Period. The police, the military, and all Civil Servants at the city, county, state, and federal level should be nonpartisan in their duties. Simply put, Unions in government are a conflict of interest, and their presence is not in the best interest of the taxpayers, the country, or the general public. And don't forget TEACHER Unions which are funded by the State and Federal taxpayers. These days it seems that the welfare of the students take a back seat to the financial interest of teachers. Unions were initially formed for good reasons, but today this writer believes that Unions have outlived their usefulness, and are only self-serving and interested in their paychecks at the expense of the public that pays higher cost for their goods and services. Unjustified public service labor strikes that halt production lines and national commerce should be limited. Would you want your Air Traffic Controller to go on strike while you're flying in mid-air? How about the fire and police? Or the military or postal service?

LIMITS ON GOVERNMENT PAY

There needs to be fair pay and good benefits and incentives in order to draw—and keep—the best career people into government service, whether it be at the city, county, state, or federal level. This pertains especially to the "workers" that make the system function efficiently for the span of their careers.

85

What it shouldn't include is the current pay system where an *elected* official is granted lifetime benefits and pay on his first day in office. Elected officials should perhaps start at a reasonable level of pay commensurate to their talent and experience (similar to entry into Civil Service), but what we see now is a system where members of Congress can vote themselves a pay raise any time they choose (as long as the pay amount isn't totally embarrassing to them and it doesn't happen in the dark of night on Christmas Eve). The pay shenanigans of Congress is way beyond what our Founding Fathers intended—that we would have career politicians in office for decades who line their pockets with the sweat of the taxpayers. But of course most of them are lawyers.

I would propose that pay raises only occur with voter approval by some means that are fair to them, and not overly costly to the taxpayer. (By the way, has anyone looked at the federal deficit lately?)

Associated with Congressional pay, I would propose that we need some Election Reform so that our hard working incumbents aren't burdened by the pressure to get elected to their next term by beginning to campaign for the next 4 to 6 years as soon as they get into office. Nationwide, campaign financing is now in the hundreds of millions to pay for elections, and the campaigning goes on for years!

New York City billionaire Michael Bloomberg spent $74 million to gain his first term as Mayor, $85 million to gain his second term, and $102 million to win a third term. That last term cost him about $174 per vote. For perspective, Donald Trump spent less than $5 per vote to win the Presidency in 2016 (*American Rifleman* magazine, May 2020),

I would propose that limits be set on how much candidates can spend so that there is a somewhat "equal opportunity" for each candidate based on his merits instead of his money, and that limits be set on the time of campaigning, say 4 to 6 months. Does money really talk for a candidate? Of course, but in some cases it doesn't; Hillary Clinton clearly outspent Trump by millions and she still lost in 2016.

Making Bills into Laws

Another Constitutional refinement into our law-making process concerns the issue of small "ear marks" that are inserted into larger packages of laws that get passed because our legislators don't want to contest them. Legislation takes time, energy, money, and compromise, and in the long run it seems easier to just pass a multi-billion-dollar bill package and get on with other business and ignore the "small" million-dollar stuff. This is how favored Senators and Congressmen get money budgeted for their particular States and districts for their pet projects, and it keeps their voting constituents happy and keeps the politician in office at reelection time. Huge airports have been built that aren't needed, "bridges to nowhere" have been built to keep workers employed, and other such items all of which are paid for by the general taxpayer. But why should the residents of Mississippi help pay for an unneeded airport in another state a thousand miles away? Why would a taxpayer in Kansas care about funding a bridge being built in Alaska? Why do powerful politicians in one state make the general taxpayers pay for their many pet "pork" projects?

Answer: Because they can.

When multiple small bills that contain a dozen various laws favoring particular states are inserted into the huge final annual Federal budget, these massive Omnibus bills get passed by the entire legislative body, even when many politicians object to the pork that wastes the taxpayers' money. It's one of the many reasons that our bloated federal deficit is out of sight, and growing larger by the day.

The solution? Ban "earmarks" and "special needs" that get bundled into large bills and passed. The $1.9 Trillion COVID bill passed in March 2021 is a perfect example. Money was allocated by the billions for all sorts of needs unrelated to the virus, and only a relatively small portion went for reparations and mitigation of the recent pandemic that closed countless businesses and put millions of people out of work.

Bills should be considered, contested, debated, and passed (or not) on the merits of just a specific bill or issue instead of inserting countless issues or needs that get buried in all the larger fluff of huge bills. Examples like this can be found in large military defense budgets, and was blatantly obvious in the "Obama Care" bill that was a disastrous failure. For Sale: Thousand-dollar toilet seats, screwdrivers, and hammers…. And what did Gun Control laws have to do with hospitals and health insurance? And who ever really reads an 800-page or 8,000-page bill before it gets voted on? Damned few people, I guarantee.

Issues and bills should be written to stand on their own before being passed into Law. It might take more time, but it would be much more fair, and understandable for people that actually take the time to read that stuff.

This is one of those issues that should be closely examined if we ever get the chance at a Convention of States.

What to Do

All talk but no action is what has gotten us to this critical point of our history, and to the conclusions of this writing.

We've touched on the issues of invasions at our borders; against Muslims both inside and outside of our country; about issues that divide our country; and of the invasions against our free speech, gun ownership, our God and our flag, sanctuary cities, the Constitution and traditional thoughts and ideas. We've touched on the controversial thoughts of what is legal vs. what is just. And issues abound that are still out there. Upon examining these few items we've asked the question WHY. Just what do we need to do to really, really, "Make America Great Again"?

The real answer concerning the Muslims is drastic, dramatic, distasteful, and destructive—economically, culturally, and politically. People will be uprooted, blood will likely be shed, and people will die. And we've heard the answer of what really needs to be done, voiced by many people, regardless of how bad and unthinkable it sounds. The harsh reality is that we're already at war, because the Muslims and Socialist Democrats have already declared it. Problem is, America seems to have ignored their declaration, no matter how clear they've made it, not once, but several times. The hijacking of the *Achille Lauro* ship; bombing of the *U.S.S. Cole*; bombing of the U.S. Marine barracks; Fort Hood—one Muslim officer killed 13, wounded 30. And what about 9-11-2001? And many other examples like ANTIFA and BLM riots and burnings.

Kill them.

Either them or us. Kill or be killed. Live standing proudly and freely in liberty, or on our knees in submission. Chose Sharia law or the U.S. Constitution. These are the hard choices that must be made—while the frog in the water is getting hotter.

How awful and brutal and inhumane the solution to the problem seems, will be screamed from the voices of Liberals the instant they read the words written on this page, without giving a nanosecond of thought as to what's happening right now, to us, *in our own country*, by the hidden enemy and open anarchists.

It's okay for Muslims to slit our throats and behead us, but it's not okay for us to do the same to them.

It's okay for them to take over our cities (been to Dearborn, MI, lately?) and impose limits around where we can go, but it's not okay for us to do the same to them.

It's okay for them to crash our airliners into multi-billion-dollar buildings and kill thousands of totally innocent people on our soil, but it's not okay for us to do the same to them.

It's okay for them to demand that we change our religion and vow to obey and support Islam or be taxed ("pay tribute") or be beheaded, but it's not okay for us to demand that they reject Islam and convert to some other religion other than Islam—ANY religion but Islam—or in turn be punished by us.

It's okay for them come to America and impose Sharia law on us, but it's not okay for us to impose our Constitutional laws on them, when they knew our customs, cultures, religion, and laws before they even came here. Or at least they should have known, if their intentions for immigrating to here were open, honorable, and forthright.

> *Honesty*: That quality we perceive in people when there is a strong correlation between what they *say* and what they *do*.

But the Muslims aren't honest and open and honorable by the very words in their Qur'an, and it drives liberals crazy that the conservatives are aware of the truth and want something done to correct the coming destruction that lies before us in the future. Same for the abject, self-declared and outspoken Socialist Democrats.

Muslim rules say to be polite and deceptive to any extent to ultimately achieve the goal of world domination and the subjugation of Infidels. But we need to fight back with the same arguments and philosophies that are destroying us. It's called You Get What You Give. We know what General George Patton said about how to win the war. And I'm reminded of the Commissioner in the *Dirty Harry* movie when the Commissioner criticized Harry that when he was out on the streets, a lot of people seemed to get shot. Harry's reply was that it was okay, as long as the right people got shot.

And we know the stand of Newt Gingrich (and millions of others): Kill Them.

The problem is how to do it, how to organize it, and who will do it.

As a start, realize that there are about 5 million registered members in the National Rifle Association (totally legal), about a hundred million gun owners not belonging to the NRA (totally legal), and probably a *couple hundred million* firearms in the homes and hands of the American population (totally legal) that have been accumulating for over three centuries since the beginning of immigrants landing on the shores of our soil. There is really no problem of a shortage of firearms. The problem is, who will fire the first shot, and who will organize the resistance to the attempted oppression of our freedoms from the illegal aliens, Muslims (foreign *and* domestic), and liberals that are bulldozing us into being a socialist country? It's been said that the biggest abuse of power is to have it and not use it when it's needed. Doesn't it seem a waste to have millions of Patriots and guns and not use them when we need to use them? We need to exercise our power now. Later will be too late. We're soft after 150 years of post-civil war peace. We know how to wage war offshore, but not at home.

And what about those anti-American socialists, both inside and outside of government, that are at the top of our economic and political food chain, i.e. Obama, Hillary, Soros, Democrat majority leaders, Hollywood, gun haters, top presidentially appointed Directors of Law Enforcement agencies like the FBI, CIA, and others?

The American military is organized for the intention of fending off invaders from foreign shores, and was not (originally) meant to solve domestic problems at home. We have seen, however, military involvement in riots to quell conflicts in the race wars of school integration in Alabama, and police actions in domestic anti-war riots during the Viet Nam era.

Personally, I can't recall when a "State Militia" was called out, even when the Blacks were burning the Watts neighborhood in L.A. in 1965, business sections of Baltimore, St. Louis, and other places, and killing cops for shooting minorities that were caught during the process of committing crimes. (Which woman Mayor made the statement, that while the place was being burned to the ground, she suggested to the police to just let the rioters burn and loot so they could just "get it out of their system?") The Rodney King riots in May 1992 resulted in property damage of $1 billion, 63 killed, 2,383 injured, and 12,000 arrests, but the State Militia wasn't called out. Instead the California Army National Guard, 7th Infantry Division, and 1st Marine Division were called. Just what would it take to call out a State Militia? And now when a militia of patriotic citizens voluntarily comes to assist in repelling an invasion of our southern border, that help from the militia is refused? Really? Again, stupid can't be cured, especially when the "stupid" resides in our own government.

What we've witnessed over the years is a gradual breakdown of our standards of law. A law that isn't enforced (or enforceable) is senseless. And many authorities in the positions to stop violence are content to just "let it run its course." The breakdown in the serious and just enforcement of our laws is a big problem mainly because those that disagree with some legal decisions publicly, politicize issues that would otherwise be cut and dried.

The uncovered coup attempt to overthrow the Trump administration was perpetrated by many of the highest law enforcement officials in our government, and only time will tell if true justice is served. Remember, most of these were Lawyers, supposedly the most honest folks in our society, but they were swayed away from their legal oaths to uphold the laws due to their liberal political bias. Interestingly, most all were Democrats.

Do you know why you should discipline the dog the very first time he gets on the living room couch? To set the precedent and teach a lesson. It does little good to wait until a week later to get the dog and kick its butt; the poor thing wonders what the hell just happened, and the only lesson the dog learns is hate for its owner. Good managers and supervisors know that infractions should be dealt with promptly, justly, and proportionally to the infraction. Same with anarchists. The old western cowboys knew this, and criminal justice was swift and sure. Onlookers at hangings learned the lesson of what happens when you break the law and as a result peace was quickly established. We've forgotten that very basic law of management and supervision, to praise in public, admonish in private, and tactfully teach employees the rules at the workplace. And teach other trivial things (like the Constitution!). We need to see justice served on those individuals that are undermining our "rule of law" no matter how high up they are on the political pole, and that justice should be served promptly.

Trump's idea to "drain the swamp" was the best political idea of our time.

Our laws need to be enforced, in all areas, and enforced at the same intensity for everyone equally, regardless of race, political, social, or economic standing. Lady Justice is blindfolded, but her blinder has slipped. We have a legal system, but what we need but don't have is a justice system. (How large or how little is another issue.) The big political talk of the day is the need for healthcare reform, but the bigger issue, is that we drastically need some reforms to our legal system. If it wasn't for the massive legal rules and regulations and endless frivolous lawsuits, our healthcare system would be better and cheaper and doctors would just be doctors, not semi-lawyers distracted by the complexities of their administrative duties. Probably a full 50% (my guess) of a hospital staff are paper pushers and support staff, rather than the highest healthcare professionals.

If we had a justice system, known murderers wouldn't be sitting on death row for twenty or thirty years waiting for their next appeal (at taxpayer expense while basking in jail), while the taxpayers keep lining the pockets of lawyers as the victims and families suffer the delays in seeing justice and closure to their pain as they also continue to be sapped financially by lawyers.

If we had a justice system, the losing parties would have to pay all the legal costs for both sides of the issues.

If we had a justice system, litigants bringing completely frivolous law suits intended to simply tie up the system would have to pay all the legal bills if they lost, including the bills of the other litigants that won their case. This would undoubtedly result in fewer court cases that are intended to delay legitimate progress on many fronts. It comes to mind that the EPA and the greenies scream and litigate every project that developers want to build these days, and tie up companies in court for so long and at such expense that the developers simply give up trying to break ground or go bankrupt. Many actions from the EPA are damaging our economy while the only people making lots of money are the lawyers.

Remember the 1700-mile-long Alaska-Canada (ALCAN) Highway that was built years ago through the most remote, wild, and hostile wilderness environment? In WWII the Japanese invaded the Aleutian Islands and were a threat to Alaska, and at that time access to Alaska was limited. So the ALCAN Highway was approved by the U.S. Army Feb. 6, 1942; construction was started on March 8, 1942, and completed Oct. 28, 1942, in only about 9 months—1700 miles, _start to finish_. Greenies and the Environmental Protection Agency (EPA) weren't around at the time, and freedom from legal encumbrances and delays made _progress_ the name of the game. Those days are gone forever. These days, just the approvals and court challenges for building even the simplest projects can take years or decades, while hard-earned capital is wasted by entrepreneurial folks trying to make an honest living. No, we shouldn't "kill all the lawyers" but sometimes the idea gives us pause to consider it, or at least urge them to reform the system. What we should do is eliminate certain government agencies that have outlived their usefulness, starting with the EPA, Dept. of Energy, and Dept. of Education.

But again, considering the abundance of firearms in the hands of honest Americans, it's a mystery as to why they haven't been called upon to quell some of these border invasions, civil internal uprisings and destructive car-burnings, business burnings, and yes, now even the attempted impeachment coup to our government by the highest officials in government. Remember, the very basic purpose for the wisdom of our founding fathers to guarantee gun ownership wasn't for hunting and recreation; it was to oppose oppression and tyranny from/by our very own government, and from enemies "both foreign _and domestic._"

Perhaps a little bit of well-planned militia anarchy would be justified to help Trump "drain the swamp."

But do we still have the "National Will" to do some of these things that must be done, like when defending our country in WWI and WWII? The current invasions discussed above are just as real and just as threatening to the future and wellbeing of America. Do we do something about it, or sit around like the frog in the pot waiting to boil? Because the role of the military is pretty well defined, the other internal sources for the defense of our country would presumably fall to the militia. Look up the definition of "militia"—it fits right in, right here. But the control of the militia is within each state, at the beck and call of the state Governors, many of which are politically liberal Democrats. Whether any, all, or none of the State Governors would ever call out the militia is unknown, so perhaps there is one more source to consider for the task of organizing the hundred million gun owners. The one entity that is somewhat immune from other governments, councils, etc., might be the County Sheriffs. Legal organization is essential, but recall that if you kill someone you're a criminal, but kill thousands and you're a hero. We might already be in that situation.

Many County Sheriffs are publicly elected, and not appointed by any other official entity, even the governor. Is it too far-fetched to think that some organization like the Association of Sheriffs could (or would) organize to bring the national invasions to an end? Leadership would be essential, and the Sheriffs are pretty autonomous from the standpoint of the independence of their office. They are the top Law Enforcement Agents in every county, elected by the local citizens, and accountable to the statutes and constitution of their state and the U.S. Constitution. Many (most?) are accountable to the voters, and are not appointed by anyone else above them.

97

Who controls the State Police? The term referring to "State Police" is as highly varied as State Trooper, Highway Patrol, State Patrol, etc., and the titles vary from State to State. These agencies are under various umbrellas named in the organization of the governing states, such as the Dept. of Highways, Dept. of Public Safety, Dept. of Transportation, etc. They are police bodies, unique to each State, and in general, they perform functions outside the jurisdiction of the County Sheriff, with some exceptions, State to State.

How about the Militia? These are generally civilian forces engaged in defense activity or service to protect a community, territory, property or laws, and generally includes the entire "able-bodied" population of a community, town, county, or state. The Militia is available to be called to arms, presumably by the Governor, or perhaps by an official over a smaller geographic or political entity such as a city or county, and not supported or sanctioned by its government, and is composed of "non-professional" soldiers and citizens that can be called upon during a time of need. And regardless of who calls out the Militia, State Police, or County Sheriff, the people concerned with preserving their freedoms can either face the challenge or slink away to some dark corner and wait for the inevitable onslaught by the invaders. We might build a wall to thwart the southern alien invaders, but the Muslim threat, present and active for almost 1400 years, is on the move and is projected to only get worse, as are our modern internal enemies.

God bless the unknown citizen that fired the first shot April 19, 1775, at the Old North Bridge at Concord, Massachusetts. The British soldiers had come to confiscate the arms of the American colonists, but this one, lone, patriotic militiaman had the prescience to realize that their disarmament by the British would be the first step in their subjugation, and the last hope of the freedoms for which they left England and Europe to attain.

Now in the face of the invasions that I have illustrated previously, and the justifications that I've stated to fight back against the invaders, I ask, WHO will organize the resistance to these invaders, both foreign <u>and</u> domestic; WHO will have the courage to shout a resounding NO to the demands of the aliens to enter our country illegally; WHO will ignore the peril of the "now" in favor of a better life for our future generations; and to achieve all these things, like the patriot at Concord, just WHO will fire the first shot?

TIMING IS EVERYTHING

President Donald Trump tried everything he could—in face of the opposition from the Democrats—to Make America Great Again.

Trump wanted to "Build the Wall" to stem the overwhelming flood of illegal aliens coming across our border, but the Democrats scream NO, seeming to care nothing about the social, medical, legal, economic, and criminal impact on Americans. And remember that we saw the news broadcast of these same Democrats in the past wholly supporting strong border security.

Trump wanted to limit or impose restrictions on immigrating Muslims, especially those coming from Syria, Iraq, Iran, and other areas of the terrorist-prone Middle East, but the Democrats scream NO, seeming to care nothing about the terrorist threat of those Muslims historically proven to be a risk to America. Democrats have short memories of how the horror on 9-11-2001 happened.

Trump supports the freedom of firearms ownership at a time when we are at risk of being overwhelmed by illegal aliens, rioters, and Muslims, but the Democrats scream NO, unwilling to accept the fact that the police can't be everywhere at once, and frankly, have little responsibility to protect everyone. The Democrats believe that a small "Gun Free Zone" sign will protect us all when the most basic logic indicates that the idea is farcical.

The Democrats totally ignored Trump's success in increasing the economy, decreasing joblessness, and his efforts to make international trade fair and equitable for the USA. Trump killed Obama's irresponsible, treasonous, ill-thought and dangerous plan to give $150 Billion to Iran, a nation that hates us and wants to build nuclear capabilities, but the Democrats screamed at that too, since it was an idea from our Muslim-sympathetic President Obama.

Trump instituted the policy that the countries belonging to the United Nations should contribute their fair share to the needs of other countries of the world instead of the USA footing the lion's share of the bill. And it doesn't matter who Trump wanted to nominate to positions for the Supreme Court, the Democrats had already prepared their vengeful speeches and justifications against his nominees even before the nominee was chosen.

And although it's crystal clear that the killing of a perfectly normal baby, as it moves along the birth canal for its first breath of air, is wanton murder, the Democrats scream that it should be the woman's choice to kill it, while Trump takes a strong Pro Life position about abortion.

Significantly, we could get back to the countless issues concerning Obama and Bill and Hillary Clinton (who the Democrats simply adore). To touch on all of their indiscretions and legal issues would take several books to write, so just recall a few words here: Benghazi; Fast & Furious; IRS targeting conservatives; NSA surveillance; Bowie Bergdahl prisoner swap; Solyndra; the Iran deal; Uranium deal; Clinton e-mail scandal; AP wiretaps; Trump Tower wiretaps; FISAgate. And how about the unexplained deaths of several Clinton associates? (All suicides, I guess....) It is now clear—crystal clear—that Joe Biden, his son Hunter, and most of the family are corrupt, and have taken what amounts to billions of dollars in payoff money for influence from the Chinese and the Ukraine. What a President he will be....

As of this writing it appears that the water already drained from Trump's swamp is starting to reveal the real bottom feeders, and most all of the mud trails are leading to the real perpetrators of all the past political uproars about Trump that have now been proven to be baseless hoaxes, i.e. Barack Obama, Joe Biden, Hillary Clinton, and all the liars and conspirators that are supported by the most wealthy Democrats. How about all the players of the Trump impeachment team that went all-out to use faulty information and lies, and failed to prove nothing illegal about Trump.

And don't forget the mainstream media and top CEOs of the social media companies that are now on special campaigns to censure information from Trump and other outspoken and influential Conservatives. Next thing you know we'll be seeing piles of books being burned in the streets.

Make no mistake about it, the label "Democrat" is clearly a cover-up for the word "Socialist." In January 2020 just before the Presidential inauguration, even the mega-rich and powerful social media companies were designing a way to censure communication specifically from Trump by permanently cancelling his internet accounts on Facebook and Twitter. If this isn't straight out of the Marxist playbook, I don't know what is. It's like Russia, North Korea, China, and other communist countries that want to control the communication media so that you hear and see only what they want you to hear and see.

Literally *everything* legal, ethical, moral, reasonable, or logical that Trump did in the best interest of America has been opposed by the Democrats. They have divided, and continue to divide, our people from coast to coast, border to border. The Democrats began a plan to impeach Trump the moment he appeared on the political scene and even had the insanity to impeach Trump again during the last week of his first term in office, and even continued *After* he left office. And Democrats say it's the Republicans that are dividing the country? About 80 million Republican voters don't think so. But don't worry, President Biden will take care of us (if he stays in office more than 6 months) or President Harris (God forbid...).

So Let's Make
America Great Again

So where do we go from here? Because of Trump's tireless pursuit of justice, the Democrat party is in shambles from all their and schemes; their lies are being exposed; and it is now time to do all the things that really, really need to be done. But unfortunately we now have a President Biden that is here at just the wrong time in our history to do all the things that Trump promised to do when he was supported by millions of conservative thinkers, and who was a thinking, logical man elected by the voters in 2016 mainly because he was <u>not</u> a career politician.

HOMELAND SECURITY

At the County level of state governments perhaps the Sheriffs are our best hope for organizing "The People" to form organized Militias. But at the <u>FEDERAL</u> level perhaps a vigorous Administrator of our Department of Homeland Security would be the perfect person to organize the millions of gun-wielding patriotic citizens willing to repel the invasions of Muslims and/or Illegal Aliens flooding across our borders. Organized Militias wouldn't take away the duties of the military that is focused on threats from outside our borders, and all it would take would be a stroke of a pen to make their activities legal, manageable, and properly directed.

Because citizen militias aren't organized, they presumably aren't "legal" or "sanctioned" so they were turned away by local officials and the FBI when they recently showed up at our southern border. A few years ago, a similar incident occurred at the Canada/Washington State border when some patriotic, gun-bearing "Minute Men" militia showed up in the wee morning hours to do a bit of house cleaning against druggies, but due to the infinite wisdom of the local authorities they too were turned away.

So we're being flooded by invaders, while many armed and capable citizens want to help protect our country, but our very own government and other officials are turning our militia away? Go figure....

Are we stupid or what? We need to organize the people that are willing to fight to defend our country.

DHS should organize and enable these red-blooded people and help our own government solve some of our problems. If one gets caught crossing the border of a country in about any other part of the world, the government AND the citizens will likely start shooting to repel invaders, but for some reason that doesn't happen at a United States border. Again, too much "legal" and not enough "justice."

"I ask, sir, what is the militia? It is the whole people except for a few public officials." —George Mason, American Patriot

The Department of "Homeland Security" needs to stand up to its namesake and HELP make our homeland secure, not work against it. DHS needs to help organize the millions of armed citizens intent on protecting America. And maybe even enlist the five million armed members of the NRA. How novel that would be…. Remember the news broadcast that showed the crowd of patriotic gun owners that spontaneously gathered in downtown Coeur d'Alene, Idaho, when the BLM/ANTIFA rioters were out to cause trouble one night? Remember that? Probably not, because the mere physical presence of the armed patriots caused the rioters to scoot off to their holes, and nothing was damaged. No news is good news.

EDUCATION

"A primary object should be the education of our youth in the science of government. In a republic, what species of knowledge can be equally important? And what duty more pressing than communicating it to those who are to be the future guardians of the liberties of the country?" –George Washington

The first thing we need to do is to start educating the masses that have been denied the proper and meaningful education about ethics, honesty, morals, religion, traditional values, and the Constitution *FOR DECADES*. This means a massive and thorough overhaul (or elimination!) of the Department of (non)Education. The retraining of the general population, and especially the Millennials, Generation Z, and the upcoming younger generation, about their socialist and entitlement mindset will take some time, so don't expect immediate results in trying to change kids immersed in a negligent system that has been deteriorating in place for almost a century. And for a variety of undisputable reasons, it should be our NATIONAL policy that ENGLISH is our first and <u>Official Language</u>. Most of the change should begin at home with the education of the *parents* who will in turn, hopefully, give a good start in educating their youngest children to patriotic and traditional values.

> *"Next in importance to freedom and justice is popular education, without which neither freedom nor justice can be permanently maintained."* —President James A. Garfield

BUILD THE WALL

The second thing to do is "Build the Wall." <u>NOW</u>. Border to border, as wide, high, and as deep as we can. We've outlined all the valid reasons in previous pages, and can't emphasize more clearly the negative impact to America of the massive influx of the hundreds, thousands, and millions of those coming over our borders of whom we know nothing about. Eliminating all those negative impacts to America will be a tremendous relief to the taxpayers in countless ways, again, already mentioned. But given the chance, President Biden will undo all of this.

ERADICATE ISLAM FROM THE U.S.A.

The next (and undoubtedly) most difficult and distasteful thing America needs to do is heart rending, and that is to get rid of the Muslims in our country. I say only in the U.S., because it is totally irrational to think that we could get rid of (about) 1.5 Billion Muslims in the rest of the world. Even the challenge and involvement of Canada and Mexico would probably be unworkable, but we could still do it in the United States if only we could summon up the ways to do it, and the National Will to do it. The Democrats and Socialists will scream from the rooftops, even at their own detriment, ignorant of the future that awaits them (and us) from not acting as soon as we can. Again, all the reasons and justifications have been previously stated.

IMPORT-EXPORT OF ALL MUSLIMS

The Muslims want to be imported into America? Well, we need to export them to countries sympathetic and welcoming to Muslims, especially all of the hard-core Muslims that refuse to convert to any other religion. Even at our expense, the cost will be cheaper now than in the future. We need to discourage them from coming to the U.S., not enable and encourage them by our INS. We need to totally restructure our immigration laws at the Immigration and Naturalization Service, especially concerning Muslims. We should _not_ allow them to build Mosques or establish boundaries around their neighborhood communities. We should make it a Federal law, with punishment and consequences, of trying to establish Sharia Laws, in any city, state, or community, right down to the last individual person. But the only LASTING solution is to rid them from the USA.

ENLIGHTENMENT OF MUSLIMS

So now what about native-born Americans that profess to the religion of Islam? A well-known belief of Muslims is that they insist that "infidels" either convert to Islam, or pay "tribute," or be beheaded.

Well, what's good for the Goose is good for the Gander too. We Americans should demand the same from them. Either _they_ convert to ANY religion other than adhere to Islam, or suffer the consequences (and also vow to make them eat pork and renounce Halal food). Given the chance they would behead us, so why shouldn't we behead them? Remember the words of General Patton. And other than decapitation, there are always incarceration or exportation as other choices. Make them make the hard choices. You (and they) should decide.

Incarceration

During the Obama administration, emails surfaced showing videos of a multitude of suspicious detention facilities being built that nobody seemed to know about, stocked with food and equipment like a detention camp. It was doubted that they were standard prison facilities for American lawbreakers, and the barbed wire and fences appeared to be designed to keep people inside, rather than from outside intrusions. This was about the time that the Obama "brown shirt" youth organizations were being formed and the conspiracy theorists believed it was for imprisoning the opponents from Obama as soon as the Muslims and Liberals took over America. These things seem to have quickly all disappeared from the internet, but the memory lingers in the minds of the Conservatives that were passing around the information and paying attention. Conspiracy theorists?

Sanctuary Cities

In addition, we need to establish STRONG Federal Laws against the idea of Sanctuary Cities that want to allow protections from Muslims, Illegal Aliens, Criminals, and Drug Addicts, in addition to those cities and municipalities that advocate unconstitutional gun bans and unreasonable restrictions on legal gun ownership and use. The anti-gun issues should be ignored and PROHIBITED at every level below the Federal Government *unless and until* the Congress changes the Second Amendment, as stated in the Constitution, and by the Constitutional _process_ for changing it. (Good luck on changing the Constitution.) A good movement towards an additional amendment to ban "sanctuary" ANYTHING should be added to the Constitution.

It amazes me that the highest levels of our government and even the Supreme Court allow the anti-gun activities of cities, states, and legislatures to abuse our gun ownership freedoms. Just who are the collective "we" that allows us to get into these situations where every municipality, small and large, wants to impose all the restrictions and regulations that predictably come flooding through the system at the turn of every election? Sanctuary Cities is the same thing—totally nonsensical and illegal, if only the elected officials in our State and Federal governments would call it what it is.

Again, we are witnessing a breakdown of the laws by those bold enough to simply ignore the law. We've all seen old movies of the Sheriff telling the cowboys coming to town that they'll have to check their firearms at the city limits. Clearly the outright confiscation is illegal and contrary to the U.S. Constitution; it might be okay for a movie, but it is clearly a way to condition the viewing public that guns are bad unless controlled by some higher authority. And if the majority of voters want their communities to be sanctuaries for people wanting to be law breakers, all it takes is one single vote over the other opposing voters. ONE VOTE, or 51% vs. 49%, can make the difference of losing freedoms and draconian impositions forced upon the losing side. One vote, or one percent makes the difference, but 49% of the people is still a very significant amount of people unhappy with the outcome. It's legal, but is it just? Right now voter tampering is a huge issue with illegal aliens voting, dead people voting, and prisoners and felons that have lost their voting rights still voting. Sounds a lot like Chicago....

Thomas Jefferson stated that Democracy is nothing more than mob rule, where 51% of the people may take away the rights of the other 49%. No wonder the sane and conservative people are fleeing many of the liberal-dominated west coast cities and states, namely California. Considering our modern times, it's a situation where it's easier for the law abusers to ask forgiveness than it is to ask for permission. Anti-gunners erode our rights without asking permission, and then, by extension, think it's the gun owners' responsibility to vote otherwise. Same with sanctuary cities. And the loss of freedoms happens slowly.

The frog in the water is getting hotter at the winning of every election by the radicals that ignore the Constitution.

MORE UNCONVENTIONAL WARFARE

So now a policeman is accused of killing a hardened black criminal named George Floyd who has a decades-old history of multiple imprisonments, theft, assault, violence, and drug use. (A coroner later determined that when arrested, Floyd was in the process of dying from drugs.) As a result of action by a policeman of this black man being televised by countless cell phones and emails along with saturation from (mostly) biased liberal newspapers and television news broadcasts, the black community gets in an uproar and stages peaceful protests all across the country. But as a great excuse to break things and cause violence in the name of Constitutionally Protected Free Speech and Rights to Assembly and Protest, organized groups quickly morph into uncontrollable mobs that are anything but peaceful. Enter BLM, ANTIFA, and its supporters and funders.

In the dark of evenings, burning and looting ensues, and the Mayors and Governors of several states order the city police to "stand down" while the rioters destroy property, raid and loot businesses, burn cars, endanger the public, and throw Molotov cocktails, bricks and clubs at the police. The result is chaos and anarchy which is discouraging to the police, many of whom choose to quit the force or retire, which leaves the cities with a neutered police force. Later, these same rioters protest to the liberal Democrat Mayors and City Councils to defund the police, which they do! (You Can't Cure Stupid.)

It begs the question of just who funds and organizes these anarchist groups. Anyone with common sense knows that the money comes from someone or some organization that is clearly anti-American and sympathetic to Marxist philosophy and Communist causes. Just how can the Mayors and Governors of some states justify holding the police back when rioting occurs? It's LEGAL (because of their powerful political positions) but is it JUST? Americans have simply become too tolerant of irresponsible authorities that have been voted into their positions by ignorant and naïve voters. Presently, the Florida governor has stated that he believes that honest citizens have the right to shoot marauding rioters caught flagrante delicto burning buildings and looting businesses. It's a good start....

The solution to civil unrest is clear: Smash it immediately and smash it hard. Call out the Police; call out the National Guard; call out the Military; and if need be, call out the millions of ready, willing, and eager public Militia that are sick of seeing anarchy go rampant and unaddressed as property is burned and businesses are destroyed. As witnessed in several cities, anarchists have tried to carve out their own enclave while local officials stand by with lots of words from their mouths and their hands in their pockets. Good people need to fight to preserve America!

Of course, authorities need to be careful about observing PEACEFUL protests, civil rights, and upholding our Constitution. But when one errant police officer mistakenly kills a citizen in an attempted legal arrest, that unfortunate act is still no free ticket for other citizens to dissolve into anarchy. Anarchy MUST be decisively crushed when it first appears or lawless activity only gets worse.

> *"Of all the dispositions and habits which lead to political prosperity, religion and morality are indispensable supports. In vain would that man claim the tribute of patriotism who should labor to subvert these great pillars of human happiness, these firmest props of the duties of men and citizens. The mere politician, equally with the pious man, ought to respect and to cherish them. Let it simply be asked, where is the security for property, for reputation, for life, if the sense of moral and religious obligation desert the oaths which are the instruments of investigation in courts of justice?"* –George Washington, Farewell address

Epilogue

The spirited contests between political parties have gone on in America for over 230 years, and although there has certainly been problems over issues and processes, our government and its public servants have worked things out, eventually, peacefully or otherwise, even if a civil war was necessary.

Our founding fathers could not possibly have foreseen the complexities of our modern life that is controlled by widespread instant communication processes, computers, incredibly complex, rapid, and deadly military systems, the marvels of the entire world created by Silicon Valley and other computerized and scientific advances, and the power of the news media and the online social media to mold and influence our social and cultural conscience.

Philosophers and Historians of the past have predicted the lifespans of cultures, and according to some, America has just about run its course, and under the (non) leadership of Obama, this country was in a freefall towards Socialism. Then Donald Trump arrested that freefall for four years and corrected a lot of problems and reversed many of the senseless policies and regulations instituted by Obama.

It's amazing that President Trump was so successful at accomplishing worthy things during his first term considering the pressures that he was under from the moment he appeared on the political scene and was nominated President. Upon the impending 2016 election of Trump, his impeachment was all planned and organized by the Democrat party just in case he won. Democrat candidate Hillary Clinton was supposed to win the election and all the machinations were set to further plunge America into the socialist picture painted by Barack Obama, right up to and including the FBI, CIA, and other intelligence agencies. Under Trump, a mission was set to "drain the swamp" but Democrat processes were set in place to thwart his efforts at every turn. The entire political establishment was upset by Trump's 2016 election.

Researchers of the 2020 elections have now uncovered countless methods of voting and balloting, both at the vote-in-person level and at the remote level of mail-in voting and computer voting. Democrats that control the mainstream media have perverted our voting processes; computerized voting machines have been loaded with biased algorithms and controllable software; and even the most trusted institutions have given the public a lot of doubt as to the honesty and integrity of our voting system.

Recent intelligence information has even transcended the Democrats in their evil effort to destroy Trump. We now know that the two brands of voting machines used all over the country (and the world) are easily manipulated to "produce the results you want" and obviously this is what happened in the several months both before _and_ after the November 2020 elections. These voting machines are built to easily access the internet, and of course if anything gets on the net, it's instantly open to the WORLD for all to see and for anyone to manipulate. And manipulate they did. The result was the first coup to destroy America. Yes, a _coup_ perpetrated by many sources across the world, has placed America in the hands of Communists across the globe. Read that again and let it soak in. A COUP? Yes.

Don't believe this? Watch the two-hour video accessed by clicking on https://michaeljlindell.com/ of how we have experienced the first not-so-secret-anymore cyber-attack on America. And it just happens that China (with love from its buddy Biden) is one of the many major international players. This 2-hour video could easily pass as a 007 James Bond spy movie, but unfortunately it's not from Hollywood, and it's sadly true. A coup to destroy America has worked. Joe Biden GOT elected, but Donald Trump WON it, by a landslide. The newly exposed personal testimony and records clearly show it. The incredible and captivation video is enlightening.

Trump WAS "draining the swamp" and the entrenched establishment took action. Trump's first term was under pressure from all directions, and whether or not the few States that held the final decisive electoral votes could be persuaded by the courts in the Blue states that were contesting the elections to give the nod to Trump wasn't to be seen. The only good that has come out of the 2020 Wuhan, China, COVID-19 pandemic virus elections, is that Trump inspired a record-setting development of an experimental vaccine.

President Donald J. Trump made it his highest priority to put America first, and his accomplishments in just his first four-year term were remarkable. As he stated in his Farewell Address on January 19, 2021, the day before the Presidential inauguration of Joe Biden, President Trump summarized the accomplishments of his administration as such:

(paraphrased) Trump ...built the greatest economy in the world; passed the largest package of tax cuts and tax reforms in history; slashed more job-killing regulations than any administration ever; withdrew from the terrible Trans-Pacific partnership and the impossible Paris Climate Accord; replaced NAFTA with the USMCA; changed many trade deals more favorable to U.S. such as renegotiating the one-sided S. Korea deal; imposed monumental tariffs on China and made great new deals with China; when the Wuhan virus pandemic hit, America still outperformed other economies; we unlocked our energy resources and became the world's number-one producer of oil and natural gas by far; achieved record jobs and lowest unemployment for all minority races and women; incomes sored, wages boomed, and millions were lifted from poverty; stock markets hit 148 highs, boosted pensions for working and retired citizens; 401(k)s were at a level as never before, both before and after the pandemic; rebuilt American manufacturing base , opened thousands of new factories, and brought back the popular phrase Made In The USA; doubled the child tax credit to ease burden on working families, and signed for largest funding ever for child care and development; joined with private sector to train more than 16 million Americans for jobs of tomorrow; inspired a medical miracle to produce two Wuhan virus vaccines in a record time of 9 months; passed economic relief package of $4 Trillion for supporting 50 million jobs, and slashed unemployment rate in half; created transparency and choices in healthcare, and got clauses added to "big pharma" for "favored nations" for lowest drug prices in the world; passed Veterans Administration rules for choice and accountability, right-to-try; landmark criminal justice reform; installed three new Justices to Supreme Court and appointed nearly 300 new Federal judges; built 450 miles of wall to make our borders the most secure in our history; gave ICE officers and border agents tools needed to do their jobs better and enforce our laws to make America safer; made security agreements with Mexico, Guatemala, Honduras, and El Salvador; restored out strength at home and leadership abroad, and built respect for America again; stood for our sovereignty at the United Nations and withdrew from the one-sided global deals adverse to our interests; made NATO nations pay $100s of billions for their fair share; put $3 Trillion towards rebuilding our military, all made in America; launched first new branch of Armed Forces in 75 years by establishing Space Force; realigned our allies to stand up to China; obliterated the ISIS Caliphate; killed top Iranian terrorists; recognized Israeli sovereignty over the Golan Heights and Jerusalem as the Capitol of Israel; achieved peace deals in Middle East—the Abraham Accord opened doors for peace; brought our soldiers home from endless Mideast wars, and Trump was first president in decades that started no new wars.

Trump's highest interest was always to the American workers and American families, and always promoted laws for safety for them.

Even after all of these accomplishments, the Leftist Democrats wanted to impeach Trump, without having substantiated legal reasons, not once, but twice, and the last attempt was as he was leaving office in the last week of his term. Then the Democrats even wanted to finalize the unprecedented and unconstitutional Senate impeachment approval AFTER Trump was out of office! The Democrats are tasteless, classless, vengeful, and hateful, and their true colors are now on display for the world to see. They want to build a dam to keep the swamp from being drained.

It appears that the Conservatives will be at war for the next four years against an incompetent Democrat as President and a dangerously socialist Vice President. If the Conservatives would have won, the BLM and ANTIFA radicals would likely have been urged into rioting against Trump; since the Democrats have won, the Conservatives will be well justified in taking up arms to right an obvious wrongful outcome of a biased, manipulated, and stolen election. God help us if Biden lets armed conflict happen, but remember, aside from Congressional funding, the President controls the military.

Biden: **I**ncreasing **D**ementia **E**ndangers **N**ation.

Especially if he is displaced by Vice President Kamala Harris before his term is completed. Her stated policies are straight from the Marxist playbook. But remember, sadly, that only the voters can put any politician in office, and it's scary that this is the complexion of the voters. They are voting for socialism, whether it be from their ignorance or their intentional political convictions.

Other people might have other ideas less drastic than what has been laid out in this writing. But will those other ideas work? I say, *only* if the ideas and appropriate actions are drastic enough; if we find a "National Will"; and if we Conservatives stop being so damned nice.

> *"The tree of liberty must be refreshed from time to time with the blood of patriots and tyrants. It is its natural manure."*
> —By Thomas Jefferson from a 1787 letter to William Stephens Smith, son-in-law of John Adams

The inauguration of Joe Biden on January 20, 2021, as our new President is now a fact, and as I glean more and more information about our current events, I run across articles from other writers that I feel are important to pass on, so I'll add a copy of an article that is supposedly written by a well-known person. However, my online research found that the "before named" author is disputed by Fact Check, so in my judgement the source should go unnamed. In any case the source is not the issue but the content, which I feel is spot on:

> "This morning, I realized that everything is about to change. No matter how I vote, no matter what I say, lives are never going to be the same.
>
> "I have been confused by the hostility of family and friends. I look at people I have known all my life so hate-filled that they agree with opinions they would never express as their own. I think that I may well have

entered the Twilight Zone. You can't justify this insanity. We have become a nation that has lost its collective mind. We see other countries going Socialist and collapsing, but it seems like a great plan to us.

"Somehow it's un-American for the census to count how many Americans are in America. People who say there is no such thing as gender are demanding a female President. Universities that advocate equality, discriminate against Asian-Americans in favor of African-Americans. Some people are held responsible for things that happened before they were born, and other people are not held responsible for what they are doing right now. Criminals are caught-and-released to hurt more people, but stopping them is bad because it's a violation of THEIR rights. People who have never owned slaves should pay slavery reparations to people who have never been slaves. After legislating gender, if a dude pretends to be a woman, you are required to pretend with him.

"It was cool for Joe Biden to 'blackmail' the President of Ukraine, but it's an impeachable offense if Donald Trump inquiries about it. People who have never been to college should pay the debts of college students who took out huge loans for their degrees. Immigrants with tuberculosis and polio are welcome, but you'd better be able to prove your dog is vaccinated. Irish doctors and German engineers who want to immigrate to the US must go through a rigorous vetting process, but any illiterate gang-bangers who jump the southern fence are welcomed.

"$5 billion for border security is too expensive, but $1.5 trillion for 'free' health care is not. If you cheat to get into college you go to prison, but if you cheat to get into the country you go to college for free. And, pointing out all this hypocrisy somehow makes us 'racists'!

"Nothing makes sense anymore, no values, no morals, no civility and people are dying of a Chinese virus, but it is racist to refer to it as Chinese even though it began in China

We are clearly living in an upside-down world where right is wrong and wrong is right, where moral is immoral and immoral is moral, where good is evil and evil is good, where killing murderers is wrong, but killing innocent babies is right.

"Wake up America. The great unsinkable ship Titanic America has hit an iceberg, is taking on water, and is sinking fast."

These are my sentiments exactly, and can serve as a synopsis of this writing. My last thought is a reminder of the decades-old cartoon character Pogo, created by Walt Kelly. Pogo thought carefully about some long-burning issues in each weekly edition of the Sunday funnies for many months, and Pogo finally concluded: "We have met the enemy, and he is US!" How apropos.

REFERENCES

I've attempted to provide all necessary references in the body of this writing, most of which are from many books I've read and from information passed to me through countless emails and other sources on the internet.

ABOUT THE WRITER

The author was born in 1942 in Wichita and raised in Kansas by hardworking blue-collar parents. As a youth he loved playing team sports, hunting, and fishing. In 1962 he joined the Navy and became a Hospital Corpsman specializing in laboratory medicine and blood banking. After being honorably discharged in 1966 off of a nuclear submarine tender harbored in Spain, he worked in Seattle as a laboratory technician while studying electronics and earned a Second Class FCC license in communication electronics. After a year working with secret clearance on a missile program at Boeing's Kent (Washington) Space Center, he attended Shoreline Community College in Seattle, achieving the Honor Roll and President's List before moving on to the University of Washington to eventually earn a Bachelor of Science degree with a minor in Math and a major in Geology. He then worked for two years for a consulting civil engineer in Seattle before being hired in 1975 by the U.S. Bureau of Mines (USBM) in Spokane where he worked as a mining and minerals field geologist on a Wilderness land evaluation program for about 11 years. From Spokane he and his wife moved to the USBM Headquarters office in Washington, D.C., where he served about five years as the Alaska Programs Manager, and was then promoted to the position of Deputy Chief of the Alaska Field Operations Center (AFOC) in Anchorage, Alaska, in the summer of 1991. Shortly afterwards, the AFOC Chief retired and the author moved into the position of Acting Chief AFOC for about two years before retiring in December 1994. The total of his post-graduate courses, work experience, social and club activities, and extensive reading during his 26 years of retirement amounts to about the equivalent of a Master's Degree in Geology and Management. While waiting for his wife to work long enough to secure some vested benefits, he worked at the Blood Bank of Alaska until moving to Blaine, Washington, in 1997. In Blaine he and his wife lived on their sailboat, designed and built their retirement house, and lived in Blaine for the next twenty years. They moved to the Southwest in late 2017. ·

The author added this personal history so that readers can evaluate the writer. He might have some strong personal opinions of what should be done to save our country, but he is not trying to influence people to get their guns and engage in uncontrolled anarchy or civil war yet.

His personal statement:

I'm a Patriot, an honorably discharged Navy veteran, and a practicing Catholic and a Fourth Degree member of the Knights of Columbus. I joined the American Legion and served on the Honor Guard for the burial ceremonies of veterans.

I've faithfully paid my taxes, on time, for the required amount, for my entire life. I'm one of the "good guys with a gun" that would readily return fire at a "bad guy with a gun" in order to save myself or family and others in a church, restaurant, or any other public place, and I've carried a sidearm and owned a concealed carry permit for about 15 years. That means that I have been fingerprinted and background checked by the FBI about six times throughout my life (and always passed clearance). I'm broadly educated and well read, and at age 79 I feel that I have the equivalent of an honorary Ph.D. in *LIFE* and have earned the privilege to write my thoughts (however eye-opening) in order to exercise my blessings and Constitutional protections under the First, Second, and all other Amendments.

In this year of 2020 and 2021, our country and the rest of the world is tainted by the Wuhan COVID-19 pandemic; we've had economic turmoil and business shutdowns, many of which are permanent; political, social, and cultural upheavals and divisions are nationwide; and extreme tension over the November 2020 national and Presidential elections has painted an uncertain future. At the moment it looks like the White House, House of Representatives, and the Senate will all be controlled by the largely leftist Democrats for at least the next two years, and unless the mid-term elections fail to move our government more to the center, probably for two additional years. If we lose our "checks and balances" in our government structure, we can only pray that God will continue to bless America in these trying times.

In my lifetime, I saw the first real overt move to Socialism when the Clintons subtly began their philosophical narrative about "politically correct" speech. Only a bit irritating and inconvenient, but be careful what you say....

The second less subtle overt move to Socialism was the leftists' outright promotion of Obama, relatively unvetted by the Democrat party; a person that had little or no political background or accomplishments; of whom we knew little about and hid his true origins; and with support of his party had the boldness to declare that he intended to "fundamentally change America." The voters naively assumed that the changes would be for the betterment of America, not its destructive transformation, and after seeing his performance for four years, those same voters had the ignorance to vote him into office yet again.

The third and most vigorous, openly hostile, and overt move to Socialism was when the Democrats began open warfare on America the moment Donald J. Trump arrived on the political scene before he was even an official candidate for President. His first term was a constant torment of hellfire from the Democrats, and even after the masses reelected him in November 2020, the leftists did everything possible to discredit the election, steal votes, enlist the social media to censure his communications, and cancel the many unprecedented accomplishments that he achieved in just his first four years. And the Democrats were successful. With the House of Representatives, the Senate, and the White House all in the hands of the leftist Democrats after the Republican losses in Georgia and several highly contested states, the smirking Senate Majority Leader Chuck Schumer chortled that "first we take Georgia, and then we transform America!" After first hearing this similar rhetoric from Obama twelve years ago, the Nation woke up and Trump supporters gathered by the thousands at the Washington, D.C., Capitol building, but the spectacle was railroaded by extremists that infiltrated the peaceful Conservative Patriots and caused the deaths of several people—and the mainstream media either failed to see through the ruse, or simply supported the effort to make Trump and his supporters look bad. This kind of drastic and alarming slide to the left has never been seen in the modern history of America, and if the courts and the voters don't correct it soon, the slide into Socialism will be irreversible. By the end of 2021 or 2022 the process of "Losing America" will likely be complete.

The main focus of this writing has been about America, but for a moment let's think internationally. A book of approximately 650 pages about pre-WWI history written by Margaret MacMillan, is *The War That Ended Peace: The Road to 1914.*

All you need to read is the 14-page Introduction in order to see the striking and disturbing similarities of our current political, cultural, ethnic, and economic National and International tensions, to the short five weeks between the assassination of Archduke Franz Ferdinand in Sarajevo on June 28th , 1914, and the outbreak of general European war that began on August 4th. The world went from peace to war in five short weeks.

We should be trembling in our boots. And remember that in 1914 there were no nuclear weapons with authorities of questionable leadership and irrational judgement holding their fingertips over the proverbial "nuclear button."

I had an exceptionally happy and satisfying upbringing by my parents, somewhat like in the nostalgic movie of *American Graffiti*, but the one regrettable thing my parents didn't teach me is the reality that we have to live in an imperfect world.